The Anger Control Workbook

By
Matthew McKay, Ph.D.
Peter D. Rogers, Ph.D.

EasyRead Large

Copyright Page from the Original Book

ReadHowYouWant partners with publishers to provide books for ALL Kinds of Readers. For more information about Becoming A RHYW Registered Reader and to find more titles in your preferred format, visit:
www.readhowyouwant.com

Publisher's Note

This publication is designed to provide accurate and authoritative information in regard to the subject matter covered. It is sold with the understanding that the publisher is not engaged in rendering psychological, financial, legal, or other professional services. If expert assistance or counseling is needed, the services of a competent professional should be sought.

This book is dedicated to all the people I've ever loved. And especially those who have loved me back.

—P.D.R.

For Noah Landis and Wendy Millstine, who've shown me a lot about having a passion for life.

—M.M.

Acknowledgment

We wish to acknowledge the extraordinary body of research by Jerry L. Deffenbacher, Ph.D., which has greatly advanced our knowledge of anger and its treatment, and is the basis of the core anger management program presented in this book.

More New Harbinger Titles

WHY ARE WE STILL FIGHTING?

Explains how our mental models about the world can short-circuit our relationships and offers strategies for effective long-term change.

TOXIC COWORKERS

This is the first guide to explain how to deal with a dysfunctional coworker who has a full-fledged personality disorder.

WORKING ANGER

This step-by-step program is designed to help anyone who has had trouble dealing with their own anger or other people's anger at work.

ANGRY ALL THE TIME

This emergency guide helps you change anger-provoking thoughts, deal with old resentments, ask for what you want without anger, and stay calm one day at a time.

LETTING GO OF ANGER

Helps you recognize the ten destructive ways that people deal with anger and identify which anger styles may be undermining your personal and work relationships.

BETTER BOUNDARIES

If you feel like you have trouble saying no to others, at work or at home, this book can help you establish more effective boundaries.

INTRODUCTION

As psychologists with a combined fifty-two years in practice, we've come to some conclusions about the problem of anger:

1. For most people, chronic anger covers incredible pain. And while anger often feels like a release at the moment, it inevitably makes the underlying pain worse.

2. Of those people who suffered the greatest damage in childhood, most were harmed by repeated exposure to anger. The majority of chronically angry people were also damaged by anger as children.

3. People struggling with chronic anger suffer long-term consequences in both work and personal relationships. They tend to feel more alone, more disappointed by life, and less nourished by their relationships.

4. The greatest predictor of satisfaction in marriage is how people learn to handle conflict and anger.

5. Anger is a learned response, and the anger response can be *unlearned* with commitment and effort.

Anger is ubiquitous in our society, from road rage to the soaring incidence of child physical abuse. Everyone is touched by it. Over the years, and tens of thousands of hours of therapy, we have seen what it costs our clients—both those who struggle with overwhelming bouts of anger, and those who are its victims. The regret, the loss, the hurt and fear leave deep scars on everyone.

Because we've seen so much pain associated with anger, we wrote, in 1989, a book called *When Anger Hurts.* The response to this book has shown us just how important the issue of anger has become. More than 200,000 copies are now in print. The book has been used as a text in anger management courses at Kaiser Permanente and the Nursing Education of America, as well as clinics and adult education programs all over North America. Hundreds of therapists regularly assign the book as homework for clients with anger problems. Many dozens of readers have contacted us to express their appreciation, and sometimes to offer suggestions for future publications.

One of the most frequent suggestions we've gotten regards the need for a step-by-step workbook that teaches anger management through a series of structured exercises. "Less theory and more practice," someone said. Another reader asked for "a sequence of skill-building exercises that teach what you need to know in the order you need to learn it."

The Anger Control Workbook has grown from these requests. This book is all about acquiring, in a step-by-step format, the skills you need to better manage anger. There are no fancy explanations, no wasted words. Just key information, along with exercises that will give you greater control over your anger response. The techniques you will learn here are proven. In study after study, relaxation techniques combined with cognitive restructuring and anger inoculation have helped to lower the frequency and intensity of anger. They will work for you too—if you commit the time and effort to actually do the exercises in this book.

The Anger Control Workbook is, unfortunately, work. It takes practice to master anger control skills. Reading won't be enough. Hoping to change won't be enough. You've already done that, and you now know that wishes and hopes are forgotten with the next outburst. You need to turn hope into action—a commitment to work your way, stepwise, through each chapter in the workbook, and to practice the new skills until they start to become second nature.

While the work won't be easy, we promise you that the reading will be. Everything you need to do is carefully and clearly explained. There are lots of examples. Worksheets help you organize your efforts, and learning is broken into small steps so nothing feels overwhelming. You will find that each chapter is set up to help you change in increments, and from the very beginning you will be given new tools to start acting differently.

Everything you need to know to overcome anger is here. Just keep reading. And working. We'll be there to help you every step of the way.

Matthew McKay
Peter D. Rogers
Calistoga, California
April 2000

CHAPTER 1

GETTING STARTED: EMERGENCY ANGER CONTROL

You're reading this book because you want to change. Chances are you're been struggling with anger for a long time, and you don't like how it affects you and those you love. Looking back, you can remember plenty of situations where you said or did things out of anger that you later wished deeply you could undo. And you've probably resolved—many times—to speak more calmly or gently, to be more understanding and less blaming, or simply to keep the lid on.

It hasn't worked. You remembered for a few hours or a few days. Then something pushed your buttons and before you knew it, all your best intentions were swept away. You may have felt guilty and bad—disgusted with yourself that your reactions seemed so automatic, so difficult to control. Perhaps you have felt helpless, watching yet another wave of anger sweep over you. It wells up in your stomach, flooding you with the need to shout and blame.

For some people, anger feels more like a cold rage, deep and poisonous. It leaks out a little at a time but never resolves, never heals. Something is terribly wrong or unfair; you feel trapped and in pain. Nothing you do seems to make it better, so the anger sets up housekeeping in your gut.

Anger isn't always about the current annoyance—this nitwit who can't take a message, or the person who cut in front of you at the toll plaza. Often the roots of anger can be traced back to earlier times when you were hurt, abused, or neglected in your family of origin. The pain was something you carried, year after year. It may have left scars so that now it's hard to feel safe or loved or truly worthy. Sometimes it doesn't take much of a provocation to trigger those feelings of being unloved, unworthy, or unsafe—and the anger rises up right alongside that old pain.

From the very start, it's important to get one thing straight. You aren't to blame because you struggle with anger. You are not a bad person because you've forgotten—perhaps repeatedly—all your resolutions to be cool and calm. Rather, you are a person in pain. Whether the pain is occasional or chronic, when it hits, it feels overwhelming. It's a wave that drives you into a state of mind where nothing matters but expressing what you feel. You shout it out. No matter who gets hurt or whatever the consequences.

Anger is a way of coping. It helps, temporarily, to overcome the hurt and helplessness. For a moment you feel back in control, and that's exactly why anger is so hard to manage. If you try to put a cork in your anger, you may feel acutely the pain that triggered it.

So now is the time to stop kicking yourself. It doesn't help. In fact, blaming yourself for your anger simply creates more pain—bad, unworthy feelings—and the pain triggers more anger. It's a self-perpetuating cycle. If you're going to get off this merry-go-round, you'll need another way to view your anger problem. Your anger is:

- A response you learned early in life to cope with pain.

- A way, however temporary, to overcome feelings of helplessness and lack of control.

- A habit that, up till now, you've lacked the tools to break.

This book will give you what you've needed but never before possessed. You will learn (1) effective, proven strategies to control angry feelings, and (2) ways to manage stress and solve problems that often fuel your anger.

Acquiring new anger management tools will take time, probably two to four months. That's the bad news. But the good news is that you *can* learn them and, in doing so, change your life. They're right here—keep reading, and keep doing the exercises. And there's more good news. While it will take time to learn your new anger management skills, there's something you can do about your anger right now—today.

Twenty-Four-Hour Commitment to Act Calm

Notice it isn't a commitment to *be* calm, just to *act* that way. Effective anger management starts with a specific, time-limited decision. You need to commit to yourself and to key people in your life that you are going to behave in a calm, nonaggressive way. Not forever. That's impossible; no one could promise such a thing. Not even for a week. That's far too long, given how strong and habitual your anger response is. Your commitment is just for a single twenty-four-hour day.

Here's how you make it work:

1. Tell people. Share with every significant person in your life that you are absolutely committed to behaving in a calm way between _____ and _____. Explain that this means you won't shout

at, swear at, hit, blame, attack, or denigrate *anyone.* Absolutely. No exceptions or excuses. Let them know that you're going to be vigilant and on guard for aggressive behavior throughout the designated time period.

2.   Ask for help. There's a good chance—especially if you experience frequent, unpredictable anger—that this won't be easy. So you need real help, not just people's good wishes. Give family and friends a nonverbal signal they can use to let you know if you're looking or sounding angry. Something like a referee's time-out sign, or the gesture an umpire uses when a player slides in safe, or just a slowly descending hand that means "relax, calm down." Whatever signal you want to use, write it in the space below and tell people how it works.

***

Prepare yourself in advance, that whenever you see the signal you will stop talking until you can once again appear calm. Remember, you don't have to *be* calm, just *act* calm.

***

3.   Sign a contract. Have one close person sign as witness to the contract below.

Twenty-Four-Hour Commitment

I _____, between _____ o'clock on _____ (date), and _____ o'clock on _____(date), promise to behave in a calm, nonaggressive manner. I will act calmly no matter what stress or provocation may occur.

_____ (Your signature)

_____ (Witness signature)

---

4. See the benefit. What's the number one thing you want to achieve through anger management? A better relationship with your spouse, your kids, your friends? A chance to heal old wounds with your family? A better shot at rewards and promotions at work? A renewed feeling of pride and self-worth? An end to dangerous or costly behavior? Whatever is your biggest and best reason for acting calm, write it in the space below:

    [Space Intentionally Left Blank in the Original Source]

5. Plan for provocations. Assume that during the twenty-four hours, things will happen to upset you. A few of them you can probably even anticipate. Write below at least four provoking events

that could threaten your commitment to calm behavior.

a. _____

b. _____

c. _____

d. _____

To face these or similar anger triggers, you'll need a few simple strategies.

What to Do When You Get Angry

First, and most important, stop. Don't do or say anything. Don't act on the angry feelings. This is just an emotion. It's a strong one, but you can feel it without turning it into behavior.

Try to step back from the feeling and label it. Notice its strength: be aware of how it pushes you toward action. Accept it. There's nothing inherently wrong with anger. It's just a signal that you're in pain. The only problem is when you act on anger to hurt others or yourself.

Don't push the feeling away, but don't try to hold onto it either. It will come like a wave—building, cresting, then slowly receding. Let it come, and then let it go. Watch how it grows and diminishes, as if you were a scientist observing some interesting phenomenon. Take care not to do anything to amplify your anger. Don't dwell on the unfairness of the situation. Don't review past failings of the offending individual. Don't rehearse in your mind the events leading to your anger. Just notice and accept the feeling, watching as it gradually diminishes.

Act the Opposite

One of the quickest ways to change a painful feeling is to act the opposite. During your twenty-four-hour commitment to calm behavior, anger can be a signal to put a very different face on your emotions.

- Smile instead of frown. The very act of smiling when angry tends to diminish the strength of your upset feelings.

- Speak softly rather than loudly. Go overboard on this. Make your voice lower and gentler than usual; try to make it soothing.

- Relax instead of tighten. Let your arms hang loose. Take a breath. Lean against something in a casual way or sit with your legs crossed comfortably. Look calm, even if you don't feel it.

- Disengage rather than attack. You may want to get right in the other person's face. You may want to shake them—emotionally if not physically. Instead, look or walk away. Make no comment about the provoking situation. Save it for another time. You'll only blow up if you try to deal with this now.

- Empathize rather than judge. Say something mildly supportive, such as, "This is a difficult situation for you," or "I can see why you're concerned (upset, overwhelmed, dismayed, etc.)." It's okay if you don't feel supportive and the words seem phony. You can have a strong desire to take a two-by-four to the other person. But just *behave* as if you can appreciate their point of view.

  "You rammed the car into the garage door? (gritting your teeth) When you're rushed, it's easy to get rattled." "You got a D+ on your math test? (rapidly growing knot in your stomach) You've been distracted, I think, but we can get back on track."

Beyond the First Twenty-four Hours

When you've gotten through the first twenty-four-hours, you have a choice. Make additional twenty-four-hour commitments (blank contracts are at the end of the chapter), or monitor your anger (using forms found in chapter 3). In either case, start working through the book to build your new anger management skills.

Notice the word "working" in the last sentence. Simply reading this book isn't enough. It will take a real effort to change such a powerful response habit. You'll need to actually complete the worksheets, exercises, and monitoring activities. And you'll need to practice your new skills every day. It's going to take time and energy, but the benefits you'll achieve by changing your angry behavior will be more than worth it.

Twenty-Four-Hour Commitment

I _____, between _____ o'clock on _____ (date), and _____ o'clock on _____ (date), promise to behave in a calm, nonaggressive manner. I will act calmly no matter what stress or provocation may occur.

_____ (Your signature)

_____ (Witness signature)

Twenty-Four-Hour Commitment

I _____, between _____ o'clock on _____ (date), and _____ o'clock on _____ (date), promise to behave in a calm, nonaggressive manner. I will act calmly no matter what stress or provocation may occur.

_____ (Your signature)

_____ (Witness signature)

Twenty-Four-Hour Commitment

I _____, between _____ o'clock on _____ (date), and _____ o'clock on _____ (date), promise to behave in a calm, nonaggressive manner. I will act calmly no matter what stress or provocation may occur.

_____ (Your signature)

_____ (Witness signature)

CHAPTER 2

THE COSTS OF ANGER

It's Thursday morning. George has been working on the Whitehorse account all week when his boss calls him into the office and tells him to drop everything and start working on the Twingle project. George feels victimized. The Twingle project is much less prestigious than the Whitehorse account. It's not fair—he was just starting to get into it, and now he's out. He's upset, and tells his boss so in no uncertain terms, storming out of the office.

On the face of it, George's anger in this situation seems justified. And his display of strong feelings might even serve to let his boss know about his degree of commitment. Perhaps the boss will realize that his decision was unfair, and change his mind.

Perhaps. But let's look at more of George's behavior to get a better perspective. This is not the first time that he's blown up at work. In fact, there have been three other episodes in the past thirty days alone. First, there was the incident with the equipment supplier, who admittedly was two days late delivering a part that George needed. Then there was the angry exchange with a coworker about who had priority using the copy machine. Worst of all was that misunderstanding with a customer who had complained to his boss. Maybe the customer was being unreasonable, his boss had said, but that was no excuse for George to be sarcastic and rude.

On further analysis, it turns out that George has lost two previous jobs because of conflicts at work, and he's received low performance evaluations for poor people skills. But the picture is even worse in his personal life. His wife filed for divorce eighteen months ago saying she couldn't stand living with him anymore. He's also been estranged from his sixteen-year-old daughter ever since he blew up and made a scene at her birthday party. And even his brother won't talk to him anymore after that incident at the bowling alley. To top it off, a recent physical found that George has high blood pressure.

Taken one at a time, each of the events referred to above might be justified or understandable. But added together, they point to a chronic anger pattern that is emotionally and physiologically damaging.

Physiological Costs of Anger

There's nothing wrong with occasional, moderate anger. It creates no lasting harm. But chronic, sustained anger can be a serious problem. By keeping the body in a constant state of emergency, chronic anger can contribute to hypertension, heart disease, and increased mortality from *all* causes. This chapter will begin by exploring what we know about how anger impacts your health. Later we'll look at the emotional and interpersonal costs of chronic anger.

Anger and Hypertension

"High" blood pressure can be understood by thinking about garden hoses. Let's say that you have two garden hoses, one a half-inch in diameter and the other a quarter-inch in diameter. If you attach the half-inch hose to the faucet and turn the valve all the way you will get a steady stream of water. However, if you attach the quarter-inch hose to the same faucet, and turn the valve all the way as before, you will get a much stronger stream. Anger is associated with high levels of norepinephrine, which tends to constrict blood vessels. This raises blood pressure as surely as if you had switched to a smaller diameter hose.

The idea that unexpressed anger (anger-in) could lead to high blood pressure has been circulating for more than half a century. In 1939, Franz Alexander suspected that his hypertensive patients were having trouble with feelings of anger and an inability to express them. This failure to express angry feelings, he argued, could lead to chronic activation of the sympathetic nervous system, and high blood pressure. Research as early as 1942, by Hamilton, confirmed that unexpressed anger was inextricably linked to hypertension. In 1982, Diamond reviewed four decades of research involving the role of anger and hostility in essential hypertension and coronary heart disease. He described the hypertensive individual as someone "ridden with hostility and constantly guarding against impulse expression." In the same year, Gentry studied the effects of habitual anger coping styles on over a thousand subjects. With this larger sample, he showed categorically that chronic suppressed anger increased the risk for hypertension.

Research by Dimsdale and associates (1986) once again confirmed that higher blood pressure is significantly related to suppressed anger. In fact, "normotensives" were twice as likely as "hypertensives" to be free of suppressed anger. All in all, there are dozens of studies linking anger-in with hypertension. You will find the most significant of these listed in the appendix.

It's clear from the research literature that the inability (or unwillingness) to express anger contributes to the development of hypertension for many susceptible people. But that's only half the story. As it turns out, people who tend to show more hostility and act more aggressively towards others (anger-out) also have higher blood pressure rates than normal.

In a 1979 study, Harburg and his associates asked people how they would deal with an angry and arbitrary boss. People's responses were categorized into three different coping strategies. The first, walking away from the situation (anger-in), was associated with people who had high blood pressure readings. The second strategy, protestation (anger-out), included behaviors such as confronting the boss or reporting him to the union. This strategy was associated with people whose blood pressure was even higher than those using the walk-away coping style. A third group used a style dubbed "reflection." These people, who said that they would try to talk to the boss later, after he had cooled down, were found to have the lowest blood pressure rates.

A host of other studies (see the Appendix for a sampling) all confirm the basic hypothesis that chronically expressed anger is associated with high blood pressure and hypertension. So it doesn't matter whether anger is suppressed or allowed to blow. Either way, your blood pressure tends to go up. It's the anger itself that's harmful, not the choice to express it or hold it back.

Anger, Hostility, and Cardiovascular Disease

In the 1950s, San Francisco cardiologists Meyer Friedman and Ray Rosenman began their seminal work on the psychosocial risk factors that underlie blocked arteries, angina pains, and heart attacks. Eventually they were able to identify a cluster of personality traits that appeared to be linked to coronary heart disease. Using the nonpejorative term "type A," they described someone who had the traits of time urgency (always in a hurry) and competitiveness. In addition, this person was highly ambitious, hyperaggressive, and experienced free-floating hostility. The type A person can be seen as someone seething with anger, always ready to boil over.

In the 1960s Friedman and Rosenman (as reported in the classic, *Type A Behavior and Your Heart,* 1974) conducted the massive Western Collaborative Group Study on 3,500 healthy men. Eighty percent of those men who had heart disease could be classified as "type A." Over the eight-and-a-half-year course of the study, type A men were twice as likely to have heart attacks as type Bs. Rosenman (1985), in his reanalysis of the Western Collaborative Group Study data, found that the anger-hostility dimension proved to be crucial. It was, in Rosenman's words, "the dominant characteristic among the coronary prone type A behaviors."

Evidence from the Western Electric Study, done by Shekelle and associates in 1983, tends to corroborate Rosenman's findings. Of the 1,877 men studied in Chicago, those who scored high on a hostility scale were one and a half times more likely to have a heart attack than men who had lower hostility scores.

Further corroboration comes from a follow-up study of 255 male physicians who completed the Hostility Scale while in medical school. Men who scored at the median or below in hostility had one-sixth the incidence of coronary heart disease twenty-five years later, compared to those who had scored higher on the scale (Barefoot et al. 1983).

Heart disease starts early for those who are chronically angry. Grunnbaum and his research group (1997) studied the association between anger or hostility and coronary heart disease in children and adolescents. Their review of epidemiological studies uncovered a strong connection between anger and pathologic changes in the arteries of young school-age children. For additional research on the relationship between hostility and coronary heart disease, see the appendix.

So far we've described research showing that the *feeling* of hostility is related to heart disease. But there is also abundant evidence that *expressed* hostility is strongly associated with coronary artery disease—*for people of all ages.* Kawachi and associates (1996) conducted a seven-year follow-up study of 1,305 men. They concluded that high levels of expressed anger are a risk factor for cardiac heart disease among older men. Siegman and associates (1987) found that expressed hostility was related to the severity of coronary artery disease in patients 60 years or younger.

The evidence is clear and overwhelming. Chronic anger and hostility can cause serious damage to your heart and arteries.

Anger, Hostility, and Death from All Causes

In 1989, the *New York Times* carried an article reporting on the results of a twenty-five-year follow-up study of law students. Among other health evaluations, the law students had taken a test measuring hostility. A striking fact emerged from this study. Twenty percent of those who had scored in the top quarter on the hostility scale were dead. This was compared to a death rate of only 5 percent for those students who had scored in the lowest quarter on the same test.

Similar results were found by Shekelle and associates in 1983. A twenty-year follow-up study of nearly two thousand initially disease-free employees of the Western Electric Company showed that high hostility scores were related to increased mortality *from all causes.*

The Finnish Twin Cohort study (Koskenvuo, et al. 1988) provides corroborating evidence from a different culture. Using a simple three-item hostility measure and a sample of 3,750 men, they found that high self-ratings of hostility were associated with increased all-cause mortality over a three-year follow-up period.

Clearly, the evidence overwhelmingly suggests that chronic anger and hostility can lead to overall poorer health, and even a likelihood of premature death.

Emotional and Interpersonal Costs of Anger and Hostility

While the physiological effects of anger, such as hypertension and artery disease, can become dramatically obvious, the emotional and interpersonal effects are more subtle. It may simply be a lonely feeling as friendships drift away. Or a sense of isolation at work because colleagues avoid making contact. Or a lack of intimacy in personal relationships as your partner becomes more guarded.

A host of studies (see the appendix) have found that high scores on hostility are associated with fewer and less satisfactory social supports. Greenglass (1996), for example, studied a sample of 252 male and 65 female managers in Canada. Those with high scores on anger-in reported receiving less support from family members. They also reported less trust in their close relationships.

Jerry Deffenbacher and his colleagues (see the appendix for a full list of research articles) have done the most extensive research on how chronic anger affects personal and work relationships. For example, Hazaleus and Deffenbacher (1986) found that 45 percent of angry males in their sample had suffered a terminated or damaged relationship during the previous year. Among other results, Deffenbacher (1992) found that angry individuals suffer significant disruptions in work or school performance, and that high anger people drink more alcohol and get drunk more often. Houston and Kelley (1989) also reported a strong relationship between anger scores and overall levels of conflict in both the family of origin and current marriages.

In 1981, Jones and his associates, found a significant relationship between hostility and loneliness. Angry people end up feeling painfully disconnected from others. When Hansson and associates reviewed the research on loneliness in 1984, they found that anger cuts people off from social support in two ways. Angry people have cynical attitudes toward others, and are therefore unable to recognize support when it's available. Similarly, their unrealistic and overly demanding expectations make the available support seem not "good enough." No matter how sincerely interested others may be in helping, the angry person is unable to experience or appreciate that support.

It's clear that angry people keep others at arm's length. In so doing, they experience less support and a greater sense of loneliness than their less hostile peers.

Assessing the Cost of Anger for You

Using the worksheets on the next page, we want you to make an honest assessment of all the ways in which anger has had a negative impact on your life. Once you have completed the exercise, it may become much clearer exactly how much anger has cost you personally. You will be ready to move on to the next chapter, which will help you to understand your anger.

PERSONAL COSTS OF ANGER—Worksheet

In the spaces provided below, write brief descriptions of how anger has affected you in each area. Put an asterisk by any numbered item that feels like a crucial reason for you to learn more about anger management.

1. How anger has affected my work relationships (include jobs lost or jeopardized):

[Space Left Intentionally Blank in the Original Source]

---

2. How anger has affected the relationships to my family of origin (including parents, siblings, and extended family):

[Space Left Intentionally Blank in the Original Source]

3. How anger has affected my marriage or intimate/romantic relationships:

[Space Left Intentionally Blank in the Original Source]

4. How anger has affected my children:

[Space Left Intentionally Blank in the Original Source]

5. How anger has affected my friendships (including lost friends and strained relationships):

[Space Left Intentionally Blank in the Original Source]

6. How my anger has harmed people who aren't family or friends (including the names of all the people my anger has hurt—on a separate sheet if necessary):

24

[Space Left Intentionally Blank in the Original Source]

7. How my anger has affected my health and physical well-being (including stress-related illnesses/problems and physical discomfort from anger reactions):

[Space Left Intentionally Blank in the Original Source]

8. How anger has endangered me (including reckless driving, physical fights, hurting myself by hitting things, legal problems, etc.):

[Space Left Intentionally Blank in the Original Source]

9. How anger has affected me financially (include bad decisions made in anger as well as material things broken or damaged):

[Space Left Intentionally Blank in the Original Source]

10. How anger has affected me spiritually (including bad behavior that goes against my personal code of ethics or sense of right and wrong):

[Space Left Intentionally Blank in the Original Source]

CHAPTER 3

UNDERSTANDING YOUR ANGER

You're reading this workbook because you're concerned about your anger. It's affecting important relationships and hurting those you care about. Perhaps it's getting you in trouble at work, while driving, or with store clerks. Maybe you're breaking things. Or it may even be affecting your health. With all the negatives associated with anger, why are you still blowing up? Why does anger remain such a powerful force in your life? Why, even when you resolve to control it, does your anger still flare up? In this chapter you'll find answers to these questions. A good place to start is understanding the five short-term payoffs that anger can provide.

Anger Payoffs

1. Anger reduces stress. Stress can come from a lot of sources—worry, frustration, unmet needs, physical pain or discomfort, rushing against deadlines, and so on. You don't need this book to tell you about your stress. What's important is the link between stress and anger. Stress creates physiological arousal—tension. The

greater the stress, and the number of stres-
sors, the more unpleasant is the arousal you
feel.

Anger discharges arousal, but only temporarily.
Right after a blowup, people often feel oddly
relaxed, like a weight has been lifted off their
shoulders. It seems like they can breathe again.
Even though these effects are brief, and tension
soon returns, the anger discharge can be
highly reinforcing. You get a break from everything that frustrates and overwhelms you.

But there's a downside to using anger for stress
reduction. The stress comes back with a
vengeance. Studies show that anger creates
more anger. Blowing up makes it more likely
that you'll blow up again soon. Each time you
indulge in anger to cope with stress, the next
outburst becomes that much easier and
stronger—and harder to control.

Not only does your anger get worse, but so
does the anger of those around you. They get
hurt and defensive. They counterattack. And
they harden, becoming less and less concerned
about your needs and feelings.

Short-term, then, anger is a good strategy for
discharging stress arousal. But it tends to

boomerang. Later, you pay dearly in the coin of broken relationships.

2.   Anger hides emotional pain. Anger is a good defense against fear, loss, guilt, shame, and feelings of rejection or failure. It puts a tight lid on painful emotions, locking most of the feelings out of awareness. Growing up in dysfunctional families, we watch Dad push away his shame with rage. Or Mom cope with her depression by yelling at the kids. We learn that we can stop virtually any painful feeling if we can just get mad enough.

But once again, the short-term payoff has long-term consequences. First of all, you don't let yourself experience feelings that may be important signals, offering guidance for what you need to do or stop doing in your life. Maybe there's a good reason you feel guilt, and you need to face it and do something about it. Maybe you need to face your depression, taking responsibility to make key changes in your life.

The second problem with using anger to defend against your feelings is that the feelings often get worse over time. You're not only guilty for some past failure—now you feel guilty for the new damage your anger has done. Or the depression worsens because your anger is turning people off and isolating you. Now you have to crank up your anger even more to block these higher levels of guilt or sadness.

The third problem with using anger as a defense is that it becomes habitual. The anger reflex seems to go off at the slightest criticism or hurt, or the slightest anxiety. Say you're a little worried while trying to figure out the bills. Boom! It's a lot easier to blow up because your partner bought a sixty-dollar espresso maker than to feel uncertainty about your finances.

3. Anger gets you attention. Sometimes it seems that no one listens to you unless you're yelling. Anger does grab people's attention. They get alarmed and sometimes they'll try to placate you. But once again, the immediate payoff has long-term outcomes that hurt you. First, a certain percentage of people don't respond to anger with attentive listening. They get immediately defensive and tune you out. They start avoiding you or, worse, they hold it against you. The problem is that you've chosen a strategy that makes some people sit up and listen, and some people run.

The second problem with using anger to get attention is that the people who responded initially get inured and hardened over time. They stop being alarmed by your anger and start being disgusted by it. Instead of listening, they resent you and shut down.

4. Anger may be used for punishment and revenge. Someone really lets you down. They screw up because they're lazy or stupid or don't care about you. Inside is this huge wave of rage. You want to punish them and teach them a lesson. You want them to feel as much pain as you do. God, it feels good. This righteousness, this will to harm, is so powerful that it's all you care about. You hunger for the opportunity to get back at them—whether it's a screamed insult or a carefully planned revenge.

    The trouble is, each time you act on these impulses, you make enemies, and the enemies often end up being the people you love and need most. Naturally, your enemies want to punish *you*. The world becomes a stage for bitter struggles, where old hurts and grudges push each of you to new excesses of rage and aggression.

5. Anger helps you change others. In dysfunctional families, we learn to use anger to extort things from others. We coerce them with blowups, or the fear of blowups, into complying with our demands. It's tempting to use anger as a club because, at least in the short term, people often give you what you want.

In the long run, of course, they turn off and turn away from you. They resent being controlled by fear. But worst of all is what it does to you. Using your anger to change others leaves you feeling helpless. When you're in pain, when something hurts, it always seems like the other person has to fix it. You feel powerless to overcome the problem yourself. And all you know how to do is try to coerce the other person into corrective action.

By placing the responsibility to change a painful situation outside yourself, you are starting down the royal slippery slope toward helplessness and depression. You're leaving others in charge of your pain and your life.

Exercise: What Are Your Anger Payoffs?

In this exercise you'll identify which of the five anger payoffs are influencing you. Don't be surprised if all or most are playing a part in your anger. For each anger payoff listed below, do a mental inventory of relationships and situations in your life (e.g., anger with family, friends, kids, coworkers, boss, clerks, receptionists; road anger; anger at objects, etc.). See if that payoff is in any way influencing or reinforcing your anger. If so, select a typical example and write it in the space provided.

1. Reduce stress—using anger to discharge stress-related arousal.

    [Space Left Intentionally Blank in the Original Source]

2. Hide emotional pain—using anger to defend against shame, guilt, depression, anxiety, and so on.

    [Space Left Intentionally Blank in the Original Source]

3. Get attention—using anger to alarm people so they'll listen to you.

    [Space Left Intentionally Blank in the Original Source]

4. Punishment and revenge—using anger to make people feel as much pain as you do.

    [Space Left Intentionally Blank in the Original Source]

5. Change the behavior of others—using anger to coerce people to do what you want.

    [Space Left Intentionally Blank in the Original Source]

You're now aware of some of the key factors that reinforce your anger and why anger has such powerful short-term effects. But there's more you need to know. To have a better chance at managing your anger, you'll need to understand the psychological mechanisms that create it. What follows is an explanation of the components of the anger response.

How You Get Angry

Anger is a two-step process. It starts with the experience of pain. The pain can be physical or emotional—it could be a stomachache or fatigue, feelings of rejection or loss. The pain can be something that frustrates your needs or threatens your safety. The particular kind of pain doesn't matter. What's important is that the pain by definition is unpleasant and makes you want to put an end to it. The second component of the anger response is trigger thoughts. These are interpretations, assumptions, and evaluations of a situation that make you feel victimized and deliberately harmed by others. Trigger thoughts blame and condemn others for the painful experience you've suffered.

You might think of emotional or physical pain as the fuel of anger. It's like a can of gasoline, and your trigger thoughts are the match. Either of the anger components alone is harmless. Pain by itself doesn't ignite rage, and trigger thoughts without pain are like a match without fuel.

Pain *plus* trigger thoughts equals anger. It's a simple formula. Imagine that you have a headache and your fourteen-year-old starts nagging you about going to a party that will involve drinking. She keeps pushing, and your head keeps pounding. Her pressure and the pain in your head aren't enough to get angry. You need a match—a trigger thought that says she's an inconsiderate kid who doesn't give a damn about how tired you are. Now the anger catches fire. You're hurting, and you have someone to blame. You've decided who's responsible for your pain. The next words out of your mouth are loud and attacking. Your daughter stares at you like you just went nuts, but in reality it was a simple matter of putting the fuel and match together.

Once you get angry, trigger thoughts can also make it worse. They can escalate your upset by continually painting the other person as bad and wrong and deliberately out to harm you. Each new trigger thought pushes your anger a notch higher, until you end up saying and doing very damaging things. Pain begets trigger thoughts, which beget anger, more trigger thoughts, more anger, and so on. Your thoughts and angry feelings become a self-perpetuating feedback loop.

Exercise: The Anger Log

The Anger Log is a tool that provides an opportunity to learn more about the components of your anger response. The log is divided into seven columns. The first column is labeled Pain/Stress; there you record the emotional and physical pain that existed before your anger. It might be a headache or anxiety about your marriage. It might be a frustrated need, or pressure to get a job done. The stress or pain might have gone on for hours preceding your anger, or it might be a direct outgrowth of the provocative situation. Try to include here every stressful or painful experience you can think of that might be influencing your anger response.

The next column is labeled Provocative Situation. Here you briefly note the upsetting event that preceded your anger. The third column, Trigger Thoughts, is where you write down what you're thinking while getting angry. These thoughts tend to label the provoking person as wrong, or bad, or harming you in some way. The fourth column is Anger Rating. Here you'll write in a number, from 0 to 100, that reflects how angry you felt. Zero would indicate no anger, whereas 100 is the highest level of rage you can imagine experiencing. When you rate each anger experience, you make a subjective judgment about where your anger falls on the continuum between those two extremes. The fifth column is labeled Behavior. Here you record what you actually *did* in response to your anger. Did you yell or speak sharply? Did you curse or call the other person names? Did you say something attacking or belittling? Were you in any way physically aggressive—shoving, shaking, hitting?

The last two columns are labeled Outcome. Here you'll note the effect of your anger on yourself and others. First of all, rate the impact from a -10 to +10 in terms of how you felt and what happened to you subsequent to your anger. Write a brief description of the emotional and objective consequences of your anger. Did you feel sad, relieved, scared? Did anything change in terms of your relationships to others? Were there consequences that you regret and that impacted you negatively? Now go through the same process in terms of how your anger may have impacted others. If you have any sense of how your anger affected them, rate it on the same -10 to +10 scale. Also note anything they said or did that appeared related to your anger.

What follows are two examples of actual Anger Logs filled out by Ginny and Ralph. Ginny is a thirty-seven-year-old X-ray technician. She's married to Bob and has a twelve-year-old son, Barry. Ralph is a fifty-one-year-old flight instructor who has a rocky relationship with his girlfriend, Laura. (Image 3.1, 3.2)

Ginny's Anger Log

Pain/Stress	Provocative Situation	Trigger Thoughts	Anger Rating 0-100	Behavior	Outcomes -10 to +10 Self	Others
1. Feeling frustrated and hurt.	Barry refuses to finish cleaning up living room during Saturday morning family work time.	He's defying me, trying to upset me. I've had enough of his lazy shit.	75	Yelled and physically pulled him back to living room.	-7 I was disgusted with myself for losing it.	-7 He pouted the rest of the day.
2. Have a headache; feeling frustrated	Ordered clothes from a catalog that came in the wrong size.	Stupid, careless people.	60	Yelled at order clerk; called her a jackass.	-2 Felt better for a moment, then depressed about how easily I lose control.	?
3. Anxious about next day dental visit for root canal; very tired	Helping Barry do homework he put off till late at night.	Same old last-minute lazy shit. He puts everything off and just assumes I'll do it.	50	Told Barry in a harsh voice that he's driving me crazy; gave him silent treatment after that.	+1 For some reason I felt like I got through to him.	-5 Barry cried.
4. Stress from deadline at work; sadness and anxiety re Bob's recent complaints about marriage.	Bob asked me to pick up some barbecue briquettes.	He knows red meat is no good for me. He doesn't give a damn about my health.	80	Told him he doesn't give a rat's ass about anything but himself.	-9 I felt very depressed.	-8 Bob stormed out to get briquettes and was yelling about divorce.
5. Sadness about state of marriage; frustrated because I wanted to go to movies but couldn't because of pain from root canal.	Bob asked about Barry's C- in English.	He leaves me with all the responsibility for Barry's schoolwork. He pays no attention.	55	Got really sharp and told him it was his own fault for ignoring the problem.	-5 Felt more depressed.	-7 Bob got really upset and left. Barry overheard and started crying. Had to comfort him.

Image 3.1

Ralph's Anger Log

Pain/Stress	Provocative Situation	Trigger Thoughts	Anger Rating 0–100	Behavior	Outcomes -10 to +10 Self	Others
1. Tired from party last night. Anxious because boss gets irritated when I'm late.	Someone cut in front of me at the bridge toll plaza.	Asshole thinks he owns the road. He needs a lesson in courtesy.	70	Shouted out the window and kept honking the horn.	-3 Felt upset and couldn't calm down.	?
2. Feel invisible, like I don't count. Old feeling from growing up.	Laura gets reservation at an Indian restaurant. Indian food burns my stomach.	It's all about her; it's all what she wants.	75	Told her to cancel reservation. Refused to go; acted very cold.	-7 Depressed, lonely. Destroying the relationship.	-5 She left in a huff, hasn't called.
3. Shame, feeling forced to do something. Also worried about money because fewer people call for flying lessons.	Mother calls from a bar drunk and wants me to drive her home.	She doesn't give a shit. She's been doing this to me too long.	90	Told her to f.o. and hung up.	+5 Felt kind of relieved and relaxed.	-3 Called her later—she hardly remembered.
4. Feeling pressured, worried about money.	Frequent flying student demands that I lower my rates.	Cheap bastard, he's got the money, he's just trying to screw me.	70	Raised my voice and told him to go find another flight instructor.	-9 Lost a student and needed income.	?
5. Feeling lonely, worried about money, kind of a hunger headache.	Laura calls last minute to say she has to work late and let's skip dinner tonight.	Doesn't give a shit about me. Just kisses up to her boss; probably doesn't have to stay. She wants to.	80	Raised voice on phone. Told her she should think about me once in a while instead of kissing up to everyone else.	-8 Very lonely and depressed.	? She laughed and said she wouldn't come home at all; hung up on me.

Image 3.2

Anger Log

Pain/Stress	Provocative Situation	Trigger Thoughts	Anger Rating 0-100	Behavior	Outcomes -10 to +10 Self	Others

Image 3.3

Now it's time to get some practice filling out your own log. On the blank Anger Log provided, fill in all the anger experiences you've had from the past week that you'd rate above 40 on the scale. If it's under 40 don't include it. Make sure you fill out the log for at least five experiences. If there weren't five in the last week, keep looking back to previous weeks until you're able to list the minimum five experiences.

As you fill out the log, be careful to differentiate between pain/stress and the provocative situation. Remember, pain/stress is what you felt physically or emotionally *before* getting angry that may have contributed to your anger response. The provocative situation is the actual event your anger focused on. Try to write down as many key trigger thoughts as possible. Later, after filling out a number of Anger Logs, you'll be able to identify themes in your trigger thoughts. When you recognize and understand the kinds of thoughts that most upset you, you'll have taken a first major step toward changing these anger triggers.

Right now, go ahead and fill in the blank Anger Log based on upsets from the past week. (Image 3.3)

Now that you've recorded at least five significant anger episodes from the past week, there are several important questions you should consider:

- What types of stresses or pain typically foreshadow high anger episodes? Are any of these stresses preventable? Could they be calmed or coped with in ways other than anger?

- What types of provocative situations are typically associated with high anger episodes? Is there a common theme or dynamic to high anger situations?

- What category of trigger thought most angers you (i.e., feeling treated unjustly, not being cared about, being ignored, blaming others, negative labels like stupid or selfish, assuming ill will, etc.)?

- Do you behave differently in response to moderate (50–60) anger as opposed to high (75–85) anger experiences? How would you like to change the way you express your anger?

- Are the outcomes more negative for high (75–85) as opposed to moderate (50–60) anger experiences?

- Are the outcomes from your anger experiences more often positive or negative? If negative, are the outcomes affecting you temporarily or also in the long term?

- Is your anger affecting others in ways that concern you?

- Are there specific trigger thoughts or trigger thought themes that seem to generate the most negative outcomes?

- Are there particular behaviors that seem to trigger more negative outcomes, either for yourself or others?

You'll return to these questions again after completing Anger Logs for the next several weeks. However, it's good to start asking them now, because careful observation of your anger helps to build motivation to complete the anger control program.

Exercise: Monitoring Your Anger

Using the blank Anger Log on the next page and making as many copies as you need, record all anger experiences over 40 on the scale during the coming week. Review your day at a consistent point each evening (for example, right at bedtime) and fill in all seven columns for all significant anger episodes. This is important work; that's why it's necessary to make a strong commitment to see it through. If you suspect you'll have difficulty maintaining the log, make a contract with a friend, and ask him or her to check in with you about your progress with the log. (Image 3.4)

Anger Log

Pain/Stress	Provocative Situation	Trigger Thoughts	Anger Rating 0-100	Behavior	Outcomes -10 to +10	
					Self	Others

Image 3.4

CHAPTER 4

RELAXATION SKILLS I

Learning to relax is an essential element in achieving anger management. Remember, getting angry is a two-step process. First, physical tension or stress has to exist in the body, then it requires anger-triggering thoughts to complete the picture. Half the anger battle can be won by simply learning to relax the physical tension that develops in provocative situations. It's a proven fact that if you can relax your body, and keep it relaxed, it's almost impossible to get angry. Combating stress using the skills you're about to learn can help you calm down, think clearly, and handle any situation in an effective, positive way. The eventual goal is to become so good at relaxing that you can let go of tension any time, anywhere, in thirty seconds or less.

The first step to effective relaxation is a technique called *progressive relaxation training.* It's been around since the 1920s in one form or another, and is generally regarded as the keystone to successful stress release. Keep in mind the technique described below is not as easy as it sounds. It requires practice and a commitment to follow through. But the results are well worth the effort, paying off big dividends in anger management.

Progressive Relaxation Training:

The basic principle is to first increase the tension in your muscles, hold it for five to seven seconds, and then *relax.* Remember to focus on one set of muscles at a time. Repeat each procedure as many times as necessary to achieve the desired effect. (*Caveat:* Do not tense areas of physical pain, injury, or recent surgery. And remove contact lenses.)

1. Get into a comfortable seated position and give your body a chance to relax. Allow yourself to experience a comfortable feeling of heaviness. Now, start at the bottom and, stretching your legs out, point your toes (like a *ballerina*) away from your body, noting the tension in your ankles. Now point your *toes to head,* creating tension in your calves. Let your feet fall to the floor, take a deep breath, and relax.

2. Now tighten your buttocks (remember *tight bottom*), and then your thighs by pressing down on your heels as hard as you can. Hold the tension (five to seven seconds), then let go, take a deep breath, and relax.

3. Take a deep breath, filling up your lungs completely, and flex your chest muscles. Now tighten your stomach muscles, creating, in effect, a *coat of armor.* Hold, then exhale, and relax.

4. Now arch your back, as though it were a bow (remember *bow and arrow*). Avoid straining and keep the rest of your body as relaxed as possible. Notice the tension beginning down at your coccyx (tailbone), and moving all the way up your spine to your neck. Hold as long as possible, then slump forward, take a deep breath, and relax.

5. Bend your elbows and tense your forearms and biceps in the classic *Charles Atlas* pose. Clench your fists at the same time. Tense these muscles until they feel taut. Then, straighten out your arms, shake out your hands, take a deep breath, and relax.

6. Now hunch your shoulders and pull your head in like a *turtle.* Press your chin against your chest, tightening your throat. Experience this uncomfortable sensation, then drop your shoulders and allow your head to fall forward. Now, slowly and carefully, roll your head to the side and back of your neck. Reverse direction and roll your head the other way. Take a deep breath, and allow your neck and shoulders to relax.

7. Continue to move your attention upwards toward your head and face. First, make a frown by wrinkling up your forehead (like a *walnut*) as tightly as you can. Next, scrunch up your eyes, flare your nostrils, clench your jaw (not so hard

that you'll crack a tooth). Finally, compress your lips into a tight O. Pull your lips as tight as a *miser's purse strings.* In short, make an *ugly face.* Hold it, tighter and tighter. Then relax and let go. Now, take a deep breath, relax your lips, and blow out forcefully.

8. Now go back mentally over the entire procedure, and feel the relaxation in your feet, ankles, calves, back, and chest. As you let go, more and more, the relaxation deepens in your neck, shoulders, arms, and hands. Go deeper and deeper into being relaxed. Finally, feel the relaxation extend to your head and face, your jaw hanging loose and your lips slightly parted.

9. If some tension persists in a specific part of your body, simply return your focus to that spot. Increase the tension, hold it, take a deep breath, and then relax. And let go.

In order to achieve deep muscle relaxation quickly, remember *key words* in the list below. Tense muscle groups for five to seven seconds, then relax for fifteen seconds.

Key Words

- Toes like a ballerina

- Toes to head

- Tight bottom

- Coat of armor

- Bow and arrow

- Charles Atlas

- Turtle

- Walnut

- Miser's purse

- Ugly face

What Does Relaxation Feel Like?

A feeling of deep relaxation can be experienced in lots of different ways. Most people describe tingling sensations, heat, or a pleasant warmth moving through their body. Others focus on feelings of heaviness or general lassitude. For some, their muscles feel like a stick of butter slowly melting in a skillet, or maple syrup spreading over a pile of pancakes. Everyone experiences relaxation in a unique way.

Exercise: How Relaxation Feels to You

Go back to the box (above) containing the key words for progressive relaxation training. As you go through the relaxation process again, notice the specific relaxation sensations that you feel for each muscle group. Now write those down next to the key words. This will serve to reinforce, and deepen, the relaxation you already experience.

Relaxation Imagery

Another very valuable tool in combating stress is the ability to call up, at a moment's notice, a peaceful, relaxing scene. Eventually, with enough practice, you will be able to conjure this scene as an automatic reflex, and it will help you to achieve better control when faced with a stressful situation.

It's best to begin using *relaxation imagery* right after having practiced the progressive relaxation procedure. This allows you to capitalize on the good feelings that you have already created. The idea is to think about, and visualize in detail, a time and place where you have felt especially safe, secure, and perfectly at peace. It sometimes helps to begin the process by imagining that you are walking down a path through the woods, with many trees on the left and right. Eventually you see a light at the end of the path, and come to a meadow. Here is a peaceful clearing, where the sun is always shining, warming your skin, and the grass smells lush. You can hear the tinkling of a brook nearby.

Perhaps it's just this meadow that you were looking for, or maybe you'll want to follow the road leading to the beach, where the waves come and go, caressing the white sand. The salty smell in the air clears your mind, and the sound of the waves lulls you into a peaceful, almost hypnotic state.

Or, you can see in the distance a cottage tucked into the side of a hill, with smoke lazily rising from the chimney. It's cozy in front of the fireplace. The smell of your favorite soup wafts from the kitchen and permeates the air, bringing back warm, nurturing memories.

Now it's time to create your own personal relaxation image. Perhaps one of the scenarios above triggered a memory for you. Or maybe a childhood scene, a time of innocence, will work for you.

Begin creating your scene slowly, with your eyes closed, sketching it in broad strokes like an artist preparing a major canvas. Visualize the scene and then anchor it to a specific time and place (e.g., 3P.M. on a lazy afternoon on August 20th, 1985, in the Catskills mountains). Now start to fill in the details. Shapes and colors, the quality of light and shadow.

Next, add the dimension of sound: blackbirds cawing as they fly overhead, or waves washing up on shore. Perhaps you can hear a faint melody, a long-forgotten tune....

Now, explore the tactile qualities of this place. Become aware of the temperature, whether it's warmth on your skin or a pleasant cool breeze. If you're lying on the grass, notice the tickling sensation as the blades brush your ear when you turn your head. And remember the unique smells associated with this time and place. Fresh mown grass, bread just out of the oven, or honeysuckle on the vine...

Finally, pay attention to the emotional "feel" of this place. Become aware of ripples of calmness, the reassuring feeling of safety and security. A sense of peace and tranquility pervades the entire scene.

When you have finished creating this peaceful scene, stop for a minute and savor the experience. Just drink it in, memorizing all the components. Let all the sights, sounds, smells, and feelings sink into your awareness. Now anchor the scene with a *key word* like "Catskills" or "Mariposa."

Open your eyes and look around. Notice where you are in the real world. Now go back to the relaxation image. Use your key word. Allow yourself to become fully immersed in the scene. See it, hear it, smell it, feel it. Notice the accompanying sense of security, peace, and relaxation. Now come back to the room again.

Use the form on the next page to record your relaxation scene. Put in as much detail as possible.

In order to help you achieve the transition from the here and now to your relaxation scene as quickly as possible, it's sometimes useful to imagine a *Magic Door.* Science fiction fans will be familiar with this concept as "teleportation," in which you are literally transported from one place to another, instantaneously. Face the nearest blank wall and picture a door with a brass knob and a brass plaque. The plaque has your key word inscribed on it. When you turn the knob and open the door, you will find, to your surprise, that your relaxation scene is already fully prepared on the other side. All you have to do is cross the threshold and there you are, safe and secure.

With a little bit of practice, you are now ready to use this relaxation scene any time there is tension, or when a situation arises that is potentially disturbing or distressing.

Summary

The two relaxation skills that you've learned in this chapter, combined with what you will learn in the next chapter, can have a major impact on your experience of anger. Progressive relaxation training, if practiced daily, can reduce overall tension. And the relaxation imagery you've created can help you face specific situations that threaten your sense of calm.

Homework

1. Using the Anger Log, continue your daily monitoring of situations that elicit anger, and be sure to note trigger thoughts. As before, all angry reactions greater than 40 (on a 100-point scale of anger arousal) are to be recorded.

2. You may photocopy the progressive relaxation training procedure and your relaxation scene in order to facilitate daily practice. Be sure to practice the relaxation training and the relaxation scene at least five times during the next week. Record all practice in the Relaxation Log.

PERSONAL RELAXATION SCENE—Worksheet

Describe time and place (where and when):

[Space Left Intentionally Blank in the Original Source]

Visual components (everything that you can see):

[Space Left Intentionally Blank in the Original Source]

Auditory components (everything that you hear):

[Space Left Intentionally Blank in the Original Source]

Tactile components (things that you touch or feel on your skin):

[Space Left Intentionally Blank in the Original Source]

Olfactory components (what you smell):

[Space Left Intentionally Blank in the Original Source]

Emotional components (feelings like safety or calmness):

[Space Left Intentionally Blank in the Original Source] (Image 4.1, 4.2)

Anger Log

Pain/Stress	Provocative Situation	Trigger Thoughts	Anger Rating 0–100	Behavior	Outcomes -10 to +10 Self	Others

Image 4.1

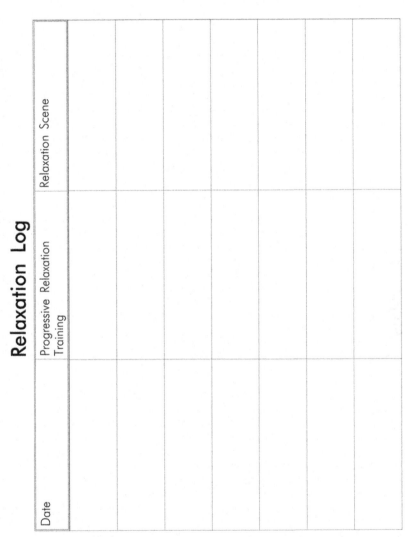

Image 4.2: INSTRUCTIONS: Put a check mark under the relaxation exercises completed on each date.

CHAPTER 5

ADVANCED RELAXATION SKILLS

Before we move on to the next set of relaxation techniques, it's useful to review the progress that you've made so far. By now you should be able to reliably relax, using the key words to follow the memorized sequence of the progressive relaxation technique. You should also be able to produce your relaxation image quickly, and in substantial detail, using all your senses. If you don't feel completely sure of yourself, practice a few more times. Then you can begin using this chapter with a sense of confidence and mastery.

At this point you may have questions about just how useful relaxation really is, especially when you find yourself in the middle of a fight with your spouse. The answer is that if you do the relaxation exercises every day, as part of your daily routine, you will notice a marked reduction in your overall tension. You'll also be less irritable. That's because relaxation has become an automatic part of your life. But this isn't enough. You need some more tools to help you relax during a period of actual upset, and that's just what this chapter is all about.

Breathing

A proper breathing technique is the next step on the relaxation agenda. Even though we've been breathing all our lives, most of us have forgotten how to breathe properly. For a quick refresher course, go find the nearest baby. Notice her little tummy rise and fall with each breath. This is called diaphragmatic, or "deep," breathing.

You can start by putting one hand on your chest and the other over your abdomen, just above the belt line. Now take a deep breath and push it all the way down into your belly. It helps to imagine filling a canteen with water. The canteen fills from the bottom up, just like the air in your belly. As you breathe in, the hand over your abdomen will rise, while the hand on your chest hardly moves at all. Focus all your attention on your belly, and send your breath down, down, down to fill your belly. Allow your breath to slightly stretch and relax your abdomen. As you take each breath, noticing your belly rise and fall, you experience a sense of calm. By doing this exercise, you are automatically sending a message to your brain that all is well. Just like a peacefully sleeping baby.

If you're having trouble pushing the air into your belly, it might be helpful to press down on your abdomen with both hands or place a moderately heavy telephone book on your abdomen. Both of these methods will not only increase your awareness, but will also force you to use your abdominal muscles.

Exercise: Deep Breathing during Stress

In order to practice *deep breathing* during stressful situations, use the outline provided on the next page. For this practice exercise, you'll need to prepare two scenes where stress can lead to a moderate anger response (but not a nuclear meltdown). Create one scene using your work environment and one scene using your home environment. Break down each situation into at least three segments. At the end of each segment is a cue to remind you to take a "deep breath." Now practice your deep breathing technique by visualizing the scenes, one segment at a time, taking a deep diaphragmatic breath at the end of each segment. Notice how the deep breath affects your tension level while you're imagining the scene.

Practice your first moderate stress scene two or three times. When you move on to the second scene, visualize it once without taking your deep breaths. Really get into it; try to make it as real as possible. Notice your stress level when you're finished. Visualize the scene at least two more times, but now taking a deep breath as you finish each segment. Chances are, you'll see that your stress level goes down when you include deep breaths during the scene.

To give you an idea of how to structure your stressful scenes on the worksheet, we've included an example worksheet with two scenes created by a forty-three-year-old insurance adjuster.

When she did this exercise, she experimented with different strategies. First she went through each scene and just thought about how it made her feel. Then she went through each scene again and did some deep breathing, as recommended. She was amazed to find how much her tension level actually went down at the end of the exercise.

Exercise: Relaxation without Tension

Up to now you've practiced the progressive relaxation technique (PRT) by increasing tension, but now it's time to eliminate that tension as well, using a technique called *relaxation without tension.* Once again, go through the PRT sequence. But this time, as you scan each muscle group, simply *notice* any tension in that part of your body, take a deep breath, and as you exhale, *relax away* and let go of all that tension.

• Start at the bottom just as before, and point your toes, then gently reverse, toes to head. Notice any tension, take a deep breath, and on the exhale, relax away the tension.

- Now focus on your buttocks. Again, just notice tension (if you find any), then take a deep breath, and on the exhale, relax.

- Next, your chest and stomach muscles. Notice, breath, exhale, relax.

- Arch your back, and, without straining, notice any tension. Then, take a deep breath, and relax away the stress.

- Focusing on your arms and biceps, simply notice any tension you may feel there. Now, take a deep breath, and on the exhale, relax the tension. Just let it go.

- Check out your neck and shoulders. Notice, breathe, exhale, relax away the tension.

- Now turn your attention to your forehead and notice any tension you may find. Move your focus to the rest of your face, and mouth. Notice any tension there, take a deep breath, and relax on the exhale.

DEEP BREATHING DURING STRESS—Worksheet

Instructions: In the spaces provided below, create two scenes that are stressful and would lead to a moderate anger response. Break each scene down into at least three segments. Fill in enough detail to allow you to fully imagine each scene. Be sure to take a deep breath at the end of each segment.

Scene 1: (work) [Space Left Intentionally Blank in the Original Source]

(deep breath)

[Space Left Intentionally Blank in the Original Source]

(deep breath)

[Space Left Intentionally Blank in the Original Source]

(deep breath)

[Space Left Intentionally Blank in the Original Source]

(deep breath)

Scene 2: (home)

[Space Left Intentionally Blank in the Original Source]

(deep breath)

[Space Left Intentionally Blank in the Original Source]

(deep breath)

[Space Left Intentionally Blank in the Original Source]

(deep breath)

[Space Left Intentionally Blank in the Original Source]

(deep breath)

DEEP BREATHING DURING STRESS—Worksheet Example

Instructions: In the spaces provided below, create two scenes that are stressful and would lead to a moderate anger response. Break each scene down into at least three segments. Fill in enough detail to allow you to fully imagine each scene. Be sure to take a deep breath at the end of each segment.

Scene 1: (work)

I'm in the car on my way to work and it's hot. The traffic is slowing down to a crawl.

(deep breath)

Now I'm literally stopped. All the windows are open, but not the hint of a breeze. A car pushes into my lane.

(deep breath)

It's a souped-up station wagon with flames painted on the side. The kid is practically hitting my fender.

(deep breath)

Heavy metal blares from his window. Now he's honking and gesturing to let him in. I won't. He keeps inching his bumper closer to my car. (deep breath)

Scene 2: (home)

> *My mother calls. High creaky vocie. Complains bit- terly about life in the same house with my aunt. Suddenly she says she wants to visit.* (deep breath)
>
> *She has the tickets already—arriving June 4. Right in the middle of finals. I tell her no way. She starts sounding irritated. Talking fast.* (deep breath)
>
> *She says the tickets aren't refundable. Accuses me of not wanting to see her, and not answering the phone when she calls. I feel hot/perspiring.* (deep breath)
>
> *She's talking really fast. I interrupt, I say my grades will suffer if she comes. She says I ought to loosen up and enjoy life; and stop bringing everyone down.* (deep breath)

Practice this at least five times before going on to the next section, and be sure to keep track by using the Relaxation Log at the end of this chapter.

Cue-Controlled Relaxation

Now it's time to choose your personal *cue word,* a two-syllable word or phrase. This will enable you to enter into a state of deep, *cue-controlled relaxation* each time you repeat it. You don't have to say it out loud. Just saying it under your breath, or even thinking it, will work just fine. Choose something like "relax," "let go," "release," or "okay." You might prefer a color, such as "deep blue," or a feeling, such as "true love." A phrase that evokes a personal memory of peace and contentment often works best.

Keeping your cue word (phrase) in mind, return your attention once again to your deep, diaphragmatic breathing. Now, each time you exhale, say your cue word (phrase) out loud or to yourself. Try to relax your entire body as you exhale, and think (or say) your cue word. Make your whole body feel as relaxed as it was when you had just finished the relaxation without tension exercise. Do this ten times in a row, to set up an automatic response pattern. Write your cue word (phrase) in the space below as a reminder:

***

Exercise: Cue-Controlled Relaxation during Stress

In order to practice this new skill, go back to the scenes you developed earlier for the deep breathing exercise. You can use the same worksheet as before—just replace the deep breathing prompt with your cue word (phrase). This will help you learn to relax by triggering the cue-controlled relaxation response, using your cue word (phrase).

Be sure to practice relaxation without tension and cue-controlled relaxation daily for the next week to ten days. Note all practice times in the Relaxation Log provided at the end of the chapter.

Combined Relaxation Skills

Once you have learned all of the essential elements of relaxation, it's time to practice them by quickly switching them on and off. For practice, do the following combinations: First, do the relaxation imagery for two minutes, followed by relaxation without tension for five minutes, and finally, cue-controlled relaxation (using deep, diaphragmatic breathing) for two minutes. Next, do the relaxation imagery again, cue-controlled relaxation, relaxation without tension, and a final round of relaxation imagery. All in all, this combined relaxation exercise will probably take no more than fifteen minutes. Practice this combined relaxation exercise at least three times in the next week (in addition to the separate relaxation without tension and cue-controlled relaxation described above). Be sure to note all practice times in the Relaxation Log. You can photocopy the sample provided to make as many sheets as you need.

Coping When You're Stressed

Everything that you've done so far is to prepare you for the "real thing." Inevitably, you'll be faced with a provocative situation in real life that challenges your resolve and threatens to blow your composure. That's why it's so important to be really comfortable with brief stress reduction strategies for anger management. This next exercise will allow you to find out for yourself exactly which strategy is most comfortable and effective for you.

Exercise: What Works for You

For this last exercise, write out another provocative scene on the worksheet provided on the next page. Be generous in your attention to detail. This will allow you to fully visualize and experience the scene so that you can *notice* where tension is concentrated in your body. Be sure to insert breathing and relaxation cues. In this exercise, relaxation without tension should focus only on the most tense part of your body. First, do a run-through of each scene without any relaxation, to determine where in your body most of the tension accumulates. Then, during relaxation without tension, you can focus only on those specific muscle groups. Alternate cue-controlled relaxation and relaxation without tension exercises. See which works best for you.

That's it. You have now learned all the key relaxation skills necessary to help control your anger and make your life less stressful. Progressive relaxation and relaxation imagery should become part of your daily routine, because they lower your overall stress and arousal level. Deep breathing, relaxation without tension, and cue-controlled relaxation can be used any time that you are faced with a provocative situation.

The key to success (How do you get to Carnegie Hall?) is practice, practice, practice. Over time these skills will become automatic, just like riding a bicycle or driving a car.

Homework

1. Continue using your Anger Log to record anger situations greater than 40 on the scale.

2. Use Relaxation Log II to note dates you practiced relaxation imagery, cue-controlled relaxation, and relaxation without tension. Plan to practice all three relaxation skills at least five out of seven days in the next week.

COPING WHEN STRESSED—Worksheet

Instructions: In the spaces provided below fill in the details of a provocative scene which is stressful and would lead to a moderate anger response. Break the scene down into 6 segments. Fill in enough detail to allow you to fully imagine the scene. Alternate deep breathing, relaxation without tension (rwt), or cue-controlled relaxation (using your cue word), at the end of each segment.

Provocative Scene:

[Space Left Intentionally Blank in the Original Source]

(deep breath) (Image 5.1, 5.2)

Anger Log

Pain/Stress	Provocative Situation	Trigger Thoughts	Anger Rating 0–100	Behavior	Outcomes -10 to +10 Self	Others

Image 5.1

Date	Relaxation Imagery	Cue-Controlled Relaxation	Relaxation without Tension

Relaxation Log II

Image 5.2: INSTRUCTIONS: Put a check mark under the relaxation exercises completed on each date.

CHAPTER 6

TRIGGER THOUGHTS

Imagine that you're in an office where several coworkers like to listen to radio talk shows at their desks. The sound isn't terribly loud, but you find yourself distracted by the constant prattle. It continues all day long. Just visualize the scene for a moment. Now imagine that you're saying to yourself, "How inconsiderate they are, how selfish, how unaware of the needs of others." Imagine yourself getting a bit worked up, thinking that they're doing this to you deliberately because they simply don't give a damn about anybody but themselves. Take a moment to notice what you are feeling.

Now imagine the scene with a little twist. Your coworkers are listening to the same distracting talk shows. This time you say to yourself, "I can't think, I can't concentrate, I'm never going to get my work done. I'm never going to get this in on time. I'm not going to be able to function here. How can I keep my job if I can't do a simple task like this when there's a little noise?" Pause a moment to notice what you're feeling.

Now imagine one last version of this scenario. Same office, same coworkers, same radio noise. On this occasion you think to yourself, "I never fit in anywhere. Things always bother me. They'll be resentful if I ask them to turn off the radio. This is the story of my life—I'm the weird one. I'm so rattle-brained that I can't even think with a little background jabber. I can't handle the slightest stress or problem." Now pause and notice what you feel with the situation framed in this way.

In the first scenario, there's a good chance that you felt a little angry. Thoughts that label others as selfish or inconsiderate, blaming them for your discomfort, tend to trigger angry feelings. The second scenario had very different thoughts. When you perceive the situation as dangerous ("I'm not going to be able to function ... how can I keep my job?"), your emotional reaction is likely to be anxiety. In the last scene, thoughts focus on self-criticism; the problems are all your fault. Your emotional response is likely to be sadness.

As you learned in chapter 2, trigger thoughts have a major impact on your anger. But anger isn't the only emotion that your thoughts influence. The above visualization suggests that thoughts can create anxiety and sadness as well. In fact, how you frame and interpret your experience has far more influence on your feelings than actual events. Your assumptions and beliefs about reality are more powerful than reality itself.

The suggestion that our own thinking might be responsible for some of our most painful emotions runs contrary to conventional wisdom. Normally, we tend to see events as the cause of our feelings, and this conception is embedded in our language. "You made me angry." "This makes me sad." "The situation scares me." But in between the event and the emotion lies your prefrontal cortex—the place in your brain where you interpret experience. It's not what actually happens that you react to, but the conclusions you draw and the assumptions you make.

Sensory Input Versus Assumptions

One way to understand the role of trigger thoughts in our emotions is to look at the distinction between sensory input (what eyes, ears, and touch tell us) and the *meanings* we create out of sensory information. In truth, we are entirely cut off from direct experience of reality. What we "see" is an internal computer screen created by our conclusions and evaluations, not a picture of the actual event.

Consider this example. Sensory input tells you a friend is frowning, her eyes are narrowing, and her voice is getting higher. She is saying something about having to rush. Because you are late for a lunch appointment, your evaluation is that she must be angry at you. That's the conclusion on your internal screen, so you begin to react defensively, perhaps even picking a fight. Only later do you learn that she was late too, had rushed to meet you, and was relieved that she hadn't kept you waiting. Here's what's important: The assumptions on your screen had almost nothing to do with reality. You'd taken a frown, narrow eyes, and an ambiguous comment and created a completely distorted picture out of them. We do this all the time. We make assumptions about the motives and feelings of others—often very wrong—and get enraged by them.

Exercise: What's on Her Screen?

The following is a transcript of a woman describing, in a psychotherapy session, a recent anger episode with her invalid mother. Read it and underline every statement that is sensory input only; then put a wavy line under every statement that comes from her screen (assumptions, conclusions, beliefs, and meanings drawn from the situation). Here's the transcript:

"She was looking at me with wide open, 'help me, help me' eyes, like she didn't care that I'd already been over there three times that week. So I said, 'What is it, Mom?' And she just sits there and doesn't say anything. She's really still. Like it's beneath her to speak the obvious, that I was put on this earth to take care of her. And I'm screwing it up. I can tell she's just disgusted with me. Finally she says, 'How about some music,' and puts on this hideous Lawrence Welk record. Which she knows I hate, and only plays when she's annoyed with me. My mother lives in passive-aggressive-ville.

"And she lies. If she says A, assume she means B. While the record is on, she says, 'All I really want is to get along with you, Carol.' But I know that's code for 'What's wrong with you, Carol, that you don't get along with me?' It's disguised criticism. That's the way she works. Then she kisses me and says all the hassling is wearing her out and she's going to take a nap before dinner. And she sort of shuffles off like I've destroyed her or something."

If you've finished doing the underlining, look ahead to see what in the transcript is sensory input, and what comes from Carol's "screen."

Sensory Input

She was looking at me with wide open eyes, so I said, "What is it, Mom?" And she just sits there and doesn't say anything. She's really still. Finally she says, "How about some music?" and puts on this Lawrence Welk record. While the record is on she says, "All I really want is to get along with you, Carol." Then she kisses me and says all the hassling is wearing her out and she's going to take a nap before dinner. She sort of shuffles off.

What's on Carol's Screen?

(She was looking at me with) "help me, help me" eyes. Like she didn't care I'd already been over there three times that week ... (She's really still) like it's beneath her to speak the obvious, that I was put on this earth to take care of her. And I'm screwing it up. I can tell she's just disgusted with me ... (she puts on) this hideous Lawrence Welk record. Which she knows I hate, and only plays when she's annoyed with me. My mother lives in passive-aggressive-ville.

And she lies. If she says A, assume she means B ... I know it's code for "What's wrong with you, Carol, that you don't get along with me?" It's disguised criticism. That's the way she works ... (she shuffles) like I've destroyed her or something.

When you separate the sensory data from the conclusions on the screen, it seems like two almost totally different experiences. In particular, the assumption, "She's just disgusted with me," appears very disconnected from what was actually said and done. In our normal thinking, sensory input and screen conclusions get folded together. The belief, "She's disgusted with me," seems every bit as real as what we actually see and hear. The trouble is that distorted conclusions on our screen often trigger big anger reactions, and we have no idea how far the assumptions on our screen are from reality.

To help distinguish sensory input from screen conclusions, you'll use a slightly modified anger log during the next week. It can be found at the end of the chapter, and it's labeled Anger Log II. It's very important, as you work toward improved anger control, to separate your thoughts (the screen) from the objective facts of a situation. Exaggeration and negative labeling are major sources of anger, and using Anger Log II will ultimately help you do less of both.

Recognizing Trigger Thoughts

You can always tell an anger-triggering thought by how it frames reality. Here are the basic components of most trigger thoughts:

1. The perception that you've been harmed and victimized.

2. The belief that the provoking person harmed you deliberately.

3. The belief that the provoking person was wrong and bad to harm you, and should have behaved differently.

Let's examine some typical trigger thoughts and see how these three elements can be separated out:

1. "Why do I have to come home from work exhausted and shop and clean and cook and get zero help?"

   Harm: Overwork, exhaustion

   Done Deliberately: Implication that the provoking person chooses not to help, thus contributing to the exhaustion.

   And Wrong: Implication that giving zero help is unjust and unfair.

2. "It's a stupid way to operate a car, and I've said it a hundred times—you don't keep riding the brakes because it wears them out."

   Harm: Cost of a brake job; not being listened to.

   Done Deliberately: Implication that if the provoking person thought a little more, or made a reasonable effort, he or she could remember to use the brakes properly.

   And Wrong: Implies that riding the brakes is poor driving technique; and not heeding appropriate warnings is either lazy or careless.

3. "She's doing this to upset me (child jumping on the sofa following an angry exchange regarding staying at the table until breakfast is eaten)."

    Harm: Noise, dirt on sofa, not being listened to.

    Done Deliberately: Implies the child is choosing obnoxious behavior out of a need for revenge.

    And Wrong: Implies child is being manipulative and disobedient.

    Now you try to identify the three elements of trigger thoughts for these next examples.

4. "How could he tell them about losing my job before I did? It's like he's trying to humiliate me."

    Harm:

    Done Deliberately:

    And Wrong:

5. "She doesn't care if the toilet flushes, just as long as I pay the rent. She's all about the money and doesn't give a damn about fixing anything."

Harm:

Done Deliberately:

And Wrong:

Answer Key for Examples 4 and 5

4. *Harm:* Humiliated; *Done Deliberately:* The provoking person chose to reveal confidential information; *And Wrong:* Implies that it's wrong to embarrass someone.

5. *Harm:* Toilet doesn't work; *Done Deliberately:* Landlord chooses to save money and ignore problem; *And Wrong:* Unfair to renters not to maintain property.

Exercise: Dissecting Your Trigger Thoughts

Take four trigger thoughts from last week's Anger Log and identify the key elements.

Trigger Thought 1
[Space Left Intentionally Blank in the Original Source]

Harm:

Done Deliberately:

And Wrong:

Trigger Thought 2
[Space Left Intentionally Blank in the Original Source]

Harm:

Done Deliberately:

And Wrong:

Trigger Thought 3
[Space Left Intentionally Blank in the Original Source]

Harm:

Done Deliberately:

And Wrong:

Trigger Thought 4
[Space Left Intentionally Blank in the Original Source]

Harm:

Done Deliberately:

And Wrong:

Trigger Thoughts Make You Feel Helpless

All trigger thoughts assert that you've been harmed, deliberately and wrongly. But there's one more implication: Not only did the provoking person cause your pain, but they ought to change so the pain can stop. They are both responsible for the harm *and* required to fix it.

The problem with this thinking is that it leaves you feeling very helpless. The pain you experience is out of your control. Someone did it to you, and you won't feel better until they see the light and change their behavior. But, as you already know*, people rarely change.* They keep behaving in habitual ways. They do what's rewarding to them, what makes them feel good. Your anger may distress them briefly, but usually they quickly return to their old patterns. The whole time you're angry, waiting for them to change, you remain stuck. You keep hurting, and the problem feels beyond your control.

This feeling of angry helplessness starts a vicious cycle: You're hurt, the provoking person should fix it but doesn't, and you feel stuck and unable to escape the pain. The feeling of helplessness makes you feel even worse, even more angry, even more frustrated that the provoking person won't change.

Breaking the cycle requires that you take responsibility for changing what's painful, and not wait for the other person to do it. For example, imagine that you have a friend who's chronically late for lunch dates. Over and over you find yourself fuming in a restaurant. Of course, you can lambaste your friend each time you find yourself stuck waiting; you can complain about the thoughtlessness and disregard for your time. However, if you take responsibility for your own pain, you might:

- always remember to bring a book and schedule extra time, or

- never meet in a restaurant, or

- always include others so you'll have someone to talk to while you wait, or

- pick your friend up at home.

Instead of being helpless and angry, you take charge of the situation. Here's another example.

Your partner never cleans up after himself. Clothes are on the floor, dishes and cups are left on the coffee table, the bathroom sink always has toothpaste residue. You can stay caught in the anger-helpless-ness-anger cycle, or you can:

- hire a weekly house cleaner at his expense;

- if there are two bathrooms, give him exclusive use of one;

- put the stuff he drops around the house on top of his desk or in a box;

- leave the dishes on his side of the bed;

- delay putting on the video till he's finished his cleanup tasks for the night;

- move out.

Think back for a moment to the situation described at the beginning of the chapter—feeling distracted by radio talk shows that coworkers listen to all day in the office. If the protagonist in the scene took responsibility for his or her own discomfort, here's how the situation might be reframed. "This is no big deal. They're having a good time. They don't know they're bugging me. I'll find a diplomatic way to get them to turn the radios down, or I'll get some headphones and listen to relaxing music." When you take responsibility, both anger and helplessness melt away. You're suddenly free to solve the problem. Instead of always asking the question, "Who's responsible for my pain?," you ask instead, "What can I do about it?"

Here are three coping mantras that can help you stay focused on taking responsibility:

1. I am responsible for what happens between us.

2. No point in blaming. I'll try a new strategy for taking care of myself.

3. What can I do about this?

Exercise: Taking Control

Review your Anger Log for the past week and complete this exercise for each provocative situation: (Image 6.1)

Here's an example of how a thirty-year-old programmer responded to this exercise: (Table 6.1)

Trigger Thought Themes

It's time to once again review the trigger thoughts you've written in your Anger Log. Now the focus should be on identifying key themes and threads that run through your anger triggers. The following is a list of typical themes that occur in trigger thoughts. Put a check by the ones that underlie some of your angry thinking.

TAKING CONTROL—Worksheet		
Provocative Situation	What I Expect from the Other Person	How I Can Take Responsibility and Control

Image 6.1

Provocative Situation	What I Expect from the Other Person	How I Can Take Responsibility and Control

1. My mother calls and asks for help paying my sister's nursing school tuition.	She ought to understand my financial situation and not embarrass me by asking for money. My sister should get a loan.	Tell her I can't help but don't reveal how truly screwed my finances are. Suggest sister get a loan that the government for-gives when you work for the VA.
2. Boss gives me a new programming assignment before I finish the one I'm working on.	He should know I'm working as fast as I can, and not load me down so I have to work all night.	Tell him I'm unable to start a new assignment till I've met my current deadline.
3. My mother arranges a birthday party for me and invites a bunch of relatives I hate.	It's crazy to make a birthday party for someone that they'll hate. She should do something I enjoy—not what she'd enjoy.	Tell her to have fun with her relatives, but that's not how I want to spend my birthday. Invite Bill and Carol and Roxanne out to dinner.
4. Roommate and her boy-friend lay all over the couch, leaving debris from a pizza, and then have a big, loud fight in the living room.	They should leave space for me to use my own living room, clean up their stuff, and fight where I can't hear it.	Tell her to clean up. Then turn up the radio in my room so I don't hear them fighting. Ask her to leave next month.

Table 6.1

_ 1. People ignore your needs.

_ 2. People don't see or understand you.

_ 3. People demand or expect too much.

_ 4. People are inconsiderate or impolite.

_ 5. People take advantage of or use you.

_ 6. People control you.

_ 7. People are selfish.

_ 8. People are stupid and thoughtless.

_ 9. People shame and/or criticize you.

_ 10. People keep you waiting.

_ 11. People are uncaring and/or ungenerous.

_ 12. People are manipulative.

_ 13. People are threatening and coercive.

_ 14. People are mean or cruel.

_ 15. People disrespect you.

_ 16. People are unfair or unjust.

_ 17. People are lazy or don't do their share.

_ 18. You're helpless and stuck and have no choice.

_ 19. People are incompetent.

_ 20. People are irresponsible.

_ 21. People don't help.

_ 22. People don't do the right thing.

Add here any additional themes you discover:

[Space Left Intentionally Blank in the Original Source]

After reviewing your Anger Log, you'll probably find that there are between two and six themes that show up with some frequency. At the root of all of the themes is the notion that people are behaving in ways they shouldn't be, and that you have a right to be angry at them for it.

But what if that weren't true? What if provoking people are doing the only thing they know how to do to take care of themselves and survive? What if they are doing the best they can, given their own needs, fears, pain, and personal history? What if people are behaving based on what they know and don't know, their skills, their physical and emotional limitations, their values, what they find most rewarding, and their available resources? The next exercise explores how most annoying and provoking behavior actually represents the other person's best coping solution, given all of the above.

Exercise: People Are Doing the Best They Can

There's a simple way to prove that this is true. Think back to something you did that really angered another person. Now write down how the following influenced your behavior and choices:

1.   Your needs at that moment:

[Space Left Intentionally Blank in the Original Source]

2.   Your fears at that moment:

[Space Left Intentionally Blank in the Original Source]

3.   Your pain or stress at that moment:

[Space Left Intentionally Blank in the Original Source]

4.   Any personal history or experiences that influenced your behavior or choices:

[Space Left Intentionally Blank in the Original Source]

5.   What you knew or didn't know at the time:

[Space Left Intentionally Blank in the Original Source]

6. Your skills or lack of skills that influenced your choice at the time:

[Space Left Intentionally Blank in the Original Source]

7. Any physical or emotional limitations that influenced you to act as you did:

[Space Left Intentionally Blank in the Original Source]

8. Personal values or beliefs that influenced your behavior:

[Space Left Intentionally Blank in the Original Source]

9. The prospects for rewards or pleasures that influenced your choice at that moment:

[Space Left Intentionally Blank in the Original Source]

10. Resources that you did or didn't have at that moment that could have influenced your choice:

[Space Left Intentionally Blank in the Original Source]

If you've really worked through this exercise, it should be clear that your behavior seemed the best available choice *at that moment.* You might, with hindsight, do something different. But it appeared to be the best response when you made it.

If you are still uncertain that you make the best choices available to you (even though they anger others), do the exercise with another situation or two. Or do it for a situation where *you* were angry, and try to identify the main influences on the other person's behavior.

A key understanding from this exercise can greatly reduce your anger response: *We are all doing the best we can to take care of ourselves.*

Homework

1. Record all anger experiences over 40 on the scale on Anger Log II. Pay careful attention to the distinction between sensory input (objective data) and the screen (your assumptions).

2. Implement at least one of the "How I can take responsibility and control" items from your Taking Control Worksheet.

3. Record practice dates for relaxation imagery, cue-controlled relaxation, and relaxation without tension on your Relaxation Log. Best results are achieved by practicing at least five out of seven days of the week. (Image 6.2, 6.3)

Anger Log II

Provocative Situation Sensory Input (Objective data from what you hear, see, and touch)	The Screen (Your conclusions, assumptions, interpretations, beliefs, and trigger thoughts)	Anger Rating 0–100	Behavior	Outcomes -10 to +10 Self	Others

Image 6.2

Relaxation Log II				
Date	Relaxation Imagery	Cue-Controlled Relaxation	Relaxation without Tension	

Image 6.3: INSTRUCTIONS: Put a check mark under the relaxation exercises completed on each date.

CHAPTER 7

THE ANGER DISTORTIONS

We know that how you think about things determines to a large degree what you experience, and this is particularly true of anger. This chapter will help you to identify the six major categories of thought distortions that are most likely to increase your feelings of anger. For each one, we've included some alternatives: new, helpful coping thoughts. The concept of coping thoughts will be explored fully in the next chapter. For now, however, it's only necessary to understand that coping thoughts are different ways of conceptualizing or reframing a situation in order to help you to better manage your anger.

Blaming

This is the most self-destructive and damaging anger distortion. The mistaken belief that underlies blaming is that other people are doing bad things to you, usually on purpose—and they aren't going to get away with it. It's true that blaming other people can make you feel better sometimes, but it leaves you feeling helpless as well. By blaming others, you are giving up the power to change the situation that is causing you pain. You keep waiting for them to change their behavior. But, of course, they never do. This can cause you to be judgmental and vindictive, lashing out angrily. The other person then responds by pulling back or counterattacking. Now you've got two problems, the original situation and the mess you've made with your angry reaction.

Examples of Blaming

- I could really enjoy this vacation if it weren't for your constant complaining and always finding fault with things.

- If you really cared about me, you would have helped me with the résumé, and then I would have gotten that job.

- You always ask me to give you a ride and then take all day to get dressed, so I'll be late for my meeting.

It's useful to remember that people are mostly doing the best they can. Everyone (including you) tends to behave in ways that will meet their own needs. The people you're blaming are most likely just doing what they can to take care of themselves as best they know how.

When you use a blaming strategy, your entire focus is on trying to change the other person. What's easy to forget is that you're not stuck. You *can* make different choices. Remember that you have some options to change the situation—it doesn't all depend on the other person. The key to dealing with self-defeating blaming is to develop a new coping strategy. This requires you to take responsibility and make your own plan to change the situation, or to figure out a different way of responding to it. Forget the other person—they're not going to do anything different. Therefore, your plan shouldn't require any cooperation whatsoever from the person you blame.

Coping Thoughts to Replace Blaming

- I know that blaming makes me feel helpless, so what can I do to change the situation and make myself feel better?

- I can make a plan to take care of myself in this situation.

- I don't like what he's doing, but I know that he's just trying to take care of himself.

- I'm hurt and disappointed, but I believe that she's doing the best she can.

- I'm not helpless, and I can take care of myself in this situation.

- They're doing what they need to do, so I'll just have to do what I need to do.

Catastrophizing/Magnifying the Situation

This is more than just making a mountain out of a molehill or making things worse than they already are. It's the tendency to take something bad and really run with it, extrapolating a bad situation to the worst possible conclusion. By magnifying events and thinking of them as awful, terrible, or horrendous, you set yourself up to respond in an angry or hostile way. In effect, you behave as though your distorted and exaggerated view of the situation were actual fact.

Examples of Catastrophizing/Magnifying:

- Because of him, my presentation is totally screwed up, and I'm going to lose my job.

- Her behavior is so disgusting that our social life is becoming a complete nightmare.

- This is the worst thing imaginable. It's all over for me now. I'll never be able to show my face around here again.

- Complete disaster! Total betrayal! How could he do something like that?

Luckily, there are a few things that you can do to control the tendency to magnify a bad situation. First, make a realistic assessment of just how bad things are. Sure, things are bad, a hassle, messed up, and definitely not the way you would like them to be. Ask yourself, "How bad is it?" Then ask yourself, "How bad is it *really?*" Make every effort to answer the second question honestly and realistically. Second, be very accurate and precise in the language you use to describe the bad situation. The restaurant bill isn't "exorbitant and outrageous," it's just a lot more than you expected. And the service wasn't a total embarrassment, the waiter was just over worked and didn't bring your soup as quickly as you have would liked.

Third, look at the whole picture, not just the annoying piece. Every situation or relationship has its positive and negative aspects. Your girlfriend may never be ready on time when you pick her up for a date. On the other hand, she's really supportive and accepting. By focusing on the positive aspects, you can neutralize your anger.

Coping Thoughts to Replace Catastrophizing

- Yeah, this is frustrating, but it's not the end of the world.

- This is really no big deal. I don't like what's going on, but it will be history next week.

- I'll get through this okay if I just hang loose.

- Wow, this situation is really messed up, but I'll do the best I can and make the most of it.

- It's only a setback. It's not worth getting all bent out of shape about it.

Inflammatory Global Labeling

This anger distortion involves making sweeping, often inflammatory, negative judgments about people whose behavior you don't like. However, instead of focusing on the behavior, the label tends to paint the person as being totally wrong, bad, and worthless. This is accomplished by one-word epithets like "loser," "asshole," "jerk," "retard," "bitch," "bastard," or "schmuck." Global labels tend to fuel your anger by turning the person whose behavior you don't like into a worthless object. And, of course the labels are always false and misleading because they reduce the whole person to a single characteristic.

Examples of Inflammatory Global Labeling

- My girlfriend is a total bitch.

- That driver who just cut me off is a complete asshole.

- What a jerk. He doesn't know anything.

- That bastard deserves to be drawn and quartered for what he did to me.

- Look at that wimpy tennis serve—he's a real loser.

The best way to combat a tendency toward global labeling is to be specific. Focus on the annoying behavior and describe it with precision. What happened? When did it happen? How often? How did it affect you or others? Notice that this does not involve making judgments about the other person or making derogatory comments about his/her personality or parentage.

Coping Thoughts to Replace Inflammatory Global Labeling

- Why am I swearing? I feel frustrated, and things aren't going the way I would like. But I can cope with the situation.

- It's nothing more than a problem. I don't have to make her the wicked witch.

- What is really bothering me? Stick to the facts.

- He's not a jerk, just someone who wasn't properly trained to do his job.

Misattributions

This is all about jumping to conclusions and mindreading. When you find yourself feeling hurt or annoyed by other people's behavior, the simplest thing is to imagine that they did it on purpose. Rather than thinking about all the other reasons for why things might have happened as they did, you assume that you know the person's "real" motives. You focus on a single explanation. They were deliberately trying to be mean to you and cause you upset.

It's easy to guess at other people's motives. But if you've ever taken the trouble to check out your assumptions, you've no doubt discovered how often you were partly or completely mistaken. Sometimes misattributions can cause real problems, such as when you angrily act on your mistaken assumptions, only to find out later that the true situation was entirely different from what you imagined.

Examples of Misattributions

- He acted like he just wanted to correct my grammar, but he was really trying to make me look stupid.

- I know she was just doing that to embarrass me in front of everyone.

- What a dumb assignment. He's really out to get me.

- The only reason she's late is just to piss me off.

The best way to avoid misattributions is to pay attention and catch yourself making the assumptions. Then, if possible, check it out with the person directly or gather some relevant facts. If you're reluctant to directly check out your assumptions, at least keep an open mind to other possibilities. Consider asking someone you trust what they make of a certain situation, to get another point of view.

Sometimes your interpretations of other people's behavior might actually be correct. However, there are usually many other reasons or explanations for people's actions—things that might surprise you. Your anger may be way out of line or disproportionate to the situation. A good way to work on misattribution is to get into the habit of developing alternative explanations for other people's behavior. Really brainstorm: Try to think of as many different scenarios as you can, and think of your original assumption as just one of many possible explanations of how other people act.

Coping Thoughts to Replace Misattributions

- That's one possibility, but there are probably other reasons for her behavior.

- Stop trying to second-guess other people's motives.

- Getting angry won't help me figure out what's really going on. I need more facts.

- My assumption may not be accurate—I'd better check it out.

Overgeneralization

Any problem can be made to look bigger or more important by using words like "never," "always," "nobody," "everybody," etc. This is a way of making an occasional occurrence feel like an intolerable ongoing event. By exaggerating, you go way beyond the truth of the situation and set yourself up for an angry response.

Examples of Overgeneralizing

- She's always doing things like that to make me look bad.

- Nobody seems to know what they're doing around here.

- You're never ready on time, so we're always late for everything.

- Everybody is always asking me to do them a favor.

The best antidote for overgeneralization is to make a conscious effort to look for exceptions. Realizing that people act in a variety of ways makes their behavior less upsetting. Ideally, you want to avoid using generalizing terms as much as possible, so it helps to use accurate and specific descriptions of the situation. For example, "This is the second time you're late this week," instead of, "you're never on time."

Coping Thoughts to Replace Overgeneralization

- No need to get upset. Just focus on the facts and I'll get through this okay.

- I want to be accurate. How often has this really happened?

- Generalizing always makes things worse. Just relax and things will calm down.

- This doesn't *always* happen this way. There are lots of exceptions.

There is a special case of overgeneralization that is worth mentioning. It's when you think in terms of black and white only, with no grays in the middle. Everything falls into one of two polar opposites: things are 100 percent right or wrong, good or bad. People either love you or hate you, with no room for anything in between. This kind of dichotomous thinking often leads to anger when people behave in less than perfect ways. Since they're not entirely right, they must be all wrong. Or, since they're not acting friendly toward you, they must be your sworn enemy.

One way of dealing with polarized thinking is to get into the habit of using qualifying adjectives and adverbs such as "a little," "a lot," or "somewhat." This will serve to reintroduce shades of gray into a black-or-white world. Another strategy is to try to see people as the complex, confusing, and often contradictory beings that they really are. By looking closely at a person you despise you may be surprised to find aspects of their personality that you like, and other aspects about which you feel at least neutral.

Demanding/Commanding

This anger distortion is best exemplified by turning your personal preferences into the equivalent of the Ten Commandments. These thoughts often involve words like "should," "got to," "have to," or "ought to." Having a well-developed sense of values is a healthy thing. However, when these values are raised to the level of moral dictates, problems with anger can occur.

Specifically, anger can often be triggered when you judge others by a set of commandments about how people should or shouldn't behave. A typical theme involves entitlement, as in, "Bad things shouldn't happen to me." Another common theme involves perfectionism, as in, "That's not the correct way to do it. You should do it the right way." Fairness is another important theme, as in, "That's not fair. It isn't right when things aren't equal."

Examples of Demanding/Commanding

- They shouldn't have done that—it was absolutely wrong.

- He isn't being fair. He should listen to me once in a while.

- She ought to have known better. That was bound to hurt my feelings.

- This is the way it's got to be. Any other way is just plain stupid.

The biggest problem with a demanding/commanding strategy is that other people rarely do what you think they should. They're too busy taking care of themselves, attending to their own wants and needs. Just because you want something or believe in something doesn't mean that others have to agree with you. This may be hard to stomach, but in fact, there's absolutely no reason why things "should" be the way that you want.

The best way to cope with "shoulds" is to reframe them as things you want or would like. These are just personal preferences. When things don't go the way you would prefer, or you don't get what you want, it's reasonable to feel frustrated and disappointed. But putting it off on someone else's moral failings is a sure road to righteous anger. You're better off sticking with desire and disappointment over shoulds and moral weakness.

Coping Thoughts to Replace Demanding/Commanding

- This is disappointing. I'd rather things were different, but I'll be all right.

- So what if I don't get what I want. It's not the end of the world, and not a reason to blow up.

- This shouldn't be happening to me. I don't like what they're doing, but I live with it.

- There's no reason why she should do it my way, other than that's the way I want it. She's got her own needs to worry about.

Now it's time to practice recognizing and dealing with anger distortions as they occur in your everyday life.

Exercise: Identifying Distortions
Using the worksheet on the next page, fill in examples from your own life of situations where you responded with each anger distortion discussed above. Focus on your thoughts in these situations, because anger distortions grow from how you think about things—your assumptions and conclusions. For example, suppose

your brother brings an uninvited guest to your Thanksgiving dinner. Your thoughts are, "He's destroying our evening, he's ruined the family feeling." This is an example of catastrophizing/magnifying and would be written into the appropriate place on the worksheet.

A complete, filled-out example follows the worksheet to help you with the exercise.

IDENTIFYING DISTORTIONS—Worksheet

Instructions: In the spaces provided below, fill in the details of anger-provoking situations in your everyday life, along with the thoughts that exemplify each anger distortion listed:

1. Blaming:

[Space Left Intentionally Blank in the Original Source]

2. Catastrophizing/magnifying:

[Space Left Intentionally Blank in the Original Source]

3. Inflammatory/global labeling:

114

[Space Left Intentionally Blank in the Original Source]

4. Misattributions:

[Space Left Intentionally Blank in the Original Source]

5. Overgeneralization:

[Space Left Intentionally Blank in the Original Source]

6. Demanding/commanding:

[Space Left Intentionally Blank in the Original Source]

IDENTIFYING DISTORTIONS—Example

Instructions: In the spaces provided below, fill in the details of anger-provoking situations in your everyday life, along with the thoughts that exemplify each anger distortion listed:

1. Blaming:

My visitation day at the park is being ruined by my kids, who keep fighting with each other and are demanding candy and popcorn. "They're always bothering me asking for stuff, so I can't enjoy the day." "If they would just stop all that bickering we could have fun."

2. Catastrophizing/magnifying:

My mother asks for help to pay a dental bill. "She's going to suck me dry."

"She's going to end up totally helpless and I'll have to take care of everything."

3. Inflammatory/global labeling:

Tim is late picking me up for a date, again. "What a complete jerk. He doesn't even know how to be on time." "He's such a loser. What am I doing with him anyway?"

4. Misattributions:

Tim is still late for the date. "The only reason that he's late is because he doesn't care about me." "I'll bet he's doing this just to annoy me."

5. Overgeneralization:

> *Waiting for my friend Mary to get ready so I can drive her to our office party. "She's never ready on time, so we're always late." "She always has some stupid excuse. Everybody we know realizes what a flake she is."*
>
> 6. Demanding/commanding:
>
> *Not happy with the way that Tim did the dishes. "That was absolutely wrong. He should have dried the wine glasses by hand." "Do it right or forget it; I'll do the damn dishes myself."*

Exercise: Correcting Distortions

Using the worksheet on the next page, name the countermeasures that you would use to combat the anger distortions that you identified in the previous exercise. Refer back to the description of each distortion to see which countermeasure might work best for you. For example, countermeasures for overgeneralizing involve: (1) looking for exceptions, (2) avoiding generalizing terms, and (3) using accurate and specific descriptions. For the anger example where you had overgeneralized, you'd choose one of these countermeasures to correct the distorted thinking.

A complete, filled-out example follows the worksheet to help you with the exercise.

Doing the exercises to identify anger distortions and name appropriate countermeasures to correct them is the first step. Next, we want you to use this information as a guide to actually revise your distorted thinking in real-life situations.

Homework

1. Continue to record anger experiences over 40 on the scale on Anger Log II. As you write down trigger thoughts in the "Screen" column, also note any anger distortions that you recognize.

2. Implement at least one more of the "How can I take responsibility and control" items form the previous chapter.

3. Using the Relaxation Log, record practice dates for relaxation imagery, cue-controlled relaxation, and relaxation without tension.

CORRECTING DISTORTIONS—Worksheet

Instructions: In the spaces provided below, name the countermeasures that you would employ for the anger distortions that you listed on the previous worksheet, then rewrite each distortion.

1. Blaming:

118

[Space Left Intentionally Blank in the Original Source]

2. Catastrophizing/magnifying:

[Space Left Intentionally Blank in the Original Source]

3. Inflammatory/global labeling:

[Space Left Intentionally Blank in the Original Source]

4. Misattributions:

[Space Left Intentionally Blank in the Original Source]

5. Overgeneralization:

[Space Left Intentionally Blank in the Original Source]

6. Demanding/commanding:

[Space Left Intentionally Blank in the Original Source]

CORRECTING DISTORTIONS—Example

Instructions: In the spaces provided below, name the countermeasures that you would employ for the anger distortions that you listed on the previous worksheet, then rewrite each distortion.

1. Blaming:

My day at the park.... Countermeasures include: (1) understand that children are doing the best they can and (2) develop a new coping strategy. New thoughts: "They're just kids, probably wanting my attention. Let's all have popcorn and enjoy ourselves."

2. Catastrophizing/magnifying:

Mother needs help with dental bill.... Countermeasures include: (1) making a realistic assessment and (2) looking at the whole picture. New thoughts: "It's just one bill, and only because she doesn't have dental coverage." "The big picture is that she has Medicare and a pension—she has her own resources."

3. Inflammatory/global labeling:

Tim is late for date.... Countermeasures include: (1) focus on the behavior and (2) avoid making derogatory judgments. New thoughts: "He's 45 minutes late. I don't like waiting, but I can handle it." "I'm not going to put him down when I don't know what happened."

4. Misattributions:

Tim is still late.... Countermeasures include: (1) avoid assumptions and (2) develop alternate explanations. New thoughts: "I'm not going to assume any thing." "He may have had car trouble or got stuck at the office."

5. Overgeneralization:

Waiting for Mary.... Countermeasures include: (1) looking for exceptions and (2) accurate and specific descriptions. New thoughts: "She's punctual maybe half the time." "She drove me to that medical test I had at the hospital—on time."

6. Demanding/commanding:

Not happy with how Tim did dishes.... Countermeasure: (1) reframe as personal preference. New thoughts: "I wish that he had dried the wine glasses by hand, but it's not the end of the world—I can live with it." (Image 7.1, 7.2)

Anger Log

Pain/Stress	Provocative Situation	Trigger Thoughts	Anger Rating 0–100	Behavior	Outcomes -10 to +10 Self	Others

Image 7.1

Relaxation Log II

Date	Relaxation Imagery	Cue-Controlled Relaxation	Relaxation without Tension

Image 7.2: INSTRUCTIONS: Put a check mark under the relaxation exercises completed on each date.

124

CHAPTER 8

CREATING COPING THOUGHTS

Congratulations, you've gotten this far in the workbook, so you've already achieved a lot. First of all, you've learned to monitor and pay attention to your anger. By itself, this is a major step in anger control. You've developed the ability to identify anger-triggering thoughts and connect them to important anger distortions. Another major achievement is learning and practicing your relaxation skills. You've rehearsed the relaxation techniques critical to anger control, and by now may be trying them out in real-life situations.

Learning to Cope with Arousal

Nearly thirty years ago, a psychologist named Donald Meichenbaum made an important observation while working with children. He noticed that while children are engaged in learning a new and challenging task, they coach themselves out loud through each step of the process. For example, a boy building an erector set structure might be heard whispering, "First I put the screw in ... washer ... hold the nut ... keep it still ... screw it tight," and soon. Meichenbaum called this kind of monologue *self-instruction.*

Self-instruction really works, but for some reason adults stop doing it. Kids learn new tasks more easily when they can talk themselves through it, and Meichenbaum wondered if adults might get the same benefit. In a series of experiments, he taught adults who suffered anxiety problems to "talk themselves through" periods of high stress. These techniques—called stress inoculation—have been very successful and are now widely used. Stress inoculation was primarily used for anxiety problems. Then a researcher named Raymond Novaco discovered that it works just as well with anger difficulties. We now call it anger inoculation, and later in this workbook you'll be using it yourself.

Just because children self-instruct out loud, you don't have to do that. You can use "coping thoughts" to remind yourself how to navigate provocative situations. When someone upsets you and you're starting to get steamed, you need to be able to remind yourself to calm down, relax, and manage your anger. What follows is a list of general coping thoughts that you can use as self-instructions whenever you find your anger escalating.

General Coping Thoughts List

- Take a deep breath and relax.

- Getting upset won't help.

- Just as long as I keep my cool, I'm in control.

- Easy does it—there's nothing to be gained in getting mad.

- I'm not going to let him/her get to me.

- I can't change him/her with anger; I'll just upset myself.

- I can find a way to say what I want to without anger.

- Stay calm—no sarcasm, no attacks.

- I can stay calm and relaxed.

- Relax and let go. There's no need to get my knickers in a twist.

- No one is right, no one is wrong. We just have different needs.

- Stay cool, make no judgments.

- No matter what is said, I know I'm a good person.

- I'll stay rational—anger won't solve anything.

- Let them look all foolish and upset. I can stay cool and calm.

- His/her opinion isn't important. I won't be pushed into losing my cool.

- Bottom line, I'm in control. I'm out of here rather than say or do something dumb.

- Take a time-out. Cool off, then come back and deal with it.

- Some situations don't have good solutions. Looks like this is one of them. No use getting all bent out of shape about it.

- It's just a hassle. Nothing more, nothing less. I can cope with hassles.

- Break it down. Anger often comes from lumping things together.

- Good. I'm getting better at this anger management stuff.

- I got angry, but kept the lid on saying dumb things. That's progress.

- It's just not worth it to get so angry.

- Anger means it's time to relax and cope.

- I can manage this; I'm in control.

- If they want me to get angry, I'm going to disappoint them.

- I can't expect people to act the way I want them to.

- I don't have to take this so seriously.

- I have a plan to relax and cope.

- This is funny if you look at it that way.

Most of the coping thoughts are focused on staying calm and relaxed. However, there's also a group of thoughts that center on keeping control and distancing yourself from the behavior of the provoking person. Right now, in the space provided, write down the three general coping thoughts that most appeal to you and seem likely to be helpful.

1. _____

2. _____

3. _____

Now take a moment to memorize the three coping thoughts you've selected. Stop. This is really important. Make a commitment that you'll use one or more of these thoughts whenever you begin to get angry during the next week. Research shows that this tool is extremely effective for maintaining control of anger and aggression.

Sometimes people find it difficult to remember to use their coping thoughts because provocations seem to erase all their good intentions. If this is likely to be a problem for you, there are some things you can do in advance to help you remember your coping thoughts. First, transfer your three coping thoughts to a piece of paper that you mount on your vanity or shaving mirror. Seeing them prominently displayed will keep them in your mind. Second, promise yourself a reward for using your coping thoughts. Especially for the first few times, you might reinforce using coping thoughts with a meal in your favorite restaurant, a new CD, a movie or video. Give yourself a treat when you succeed in remembering, regardless of whether you fully control your anger. Right now, remembering and making an effort are enough. Third, tell a friend about your effort to use coping thoughts, and ask him or her to check in with you to see if you're remembering them. Fourth, use a physical cue. It might help this week to wear a new or unusual piece of jewelry that's associated with your plan to use coping thoughts. Another option is to wear your watch on the wrong wrist or unusual shoes or a sweater you don't particularly like—anything that will remind you of your new effort to cope.

Perhaps the best strategy to help you remember your coping thoughts is to plan in advance for provoking situations. For example, if your kids dawdle most mornings getting ready for school, plan out exactly when and how you'll use your coping thoughts. First, you'll want to plan for a cue or reminder in the situation. In the case of slow-moving kids, you might want to place one or more of your coping thoughts on a sign near the kitchen table. Or you might put something strange and inappropriate on the table (your daughter's wire sculpture of a horsefly), so you're cued to cope. A second step in planning involves identifying a clear behavioral indicator that tells you to start managing your anger. It might be when you raise your voice, or start pushing the kids down in their chairs, or make particular attacking comments. A third stage in planning is to identify exactly *how* you will cope. For example, you might decide to take a deep breath and use your cue word, then tell yourself, "Easy does it—there's nothing to be gained in getting mad." The *how* of coping might also include walking out of the room for a minute so you can breathe and use your coping thoughts away from the children.

Exercise: Making a Coping Plan

This exercise will help you plan a coping response for one anger-provoking situation that's likely to occur in the next week. Start by identifying the situation, including enough details so you're clear about the exact set of circumstances that you're planning for. Then identify one or more cues to remind you of your coping thoughts and plan. Make sure that the cues will be present and prominent in the situation where your anger is likely to be triggered. Next, under When to Cope, write down the behavioral red flags that tell you it's time to deal with your anger. Whether it's criticizing or pointing your finger or laughing sarcastically, the red flag should be specific to the situation you're planning for. Finally, under How to Cope, note the specific coping thoughts you plan to use and any actions you want to take to keep your anger from escalating. Always include one of the relaxation strategies that's quick and easy to use as part of your How to Cope plan.

Coping Plan
1.   Situation

[Space Left Intentionally Blank in the Original Source]

2.   Cues to Cope

[Space Left Intentionally Blank in the Original Source]

3.   When to Cope

[Space Left Intentionally Blank in the Original Source]

4.   How to Cope

[Space Left Intentionally Blank in the Original Source]

Coping Thoughts for Prolonged Anger or Anger Distortions

Sometimes general coping thoughts aren't enough. You're too angry, or the situation is triggering anger distortions that inflame your feelings. Controlling anger in these cases requires more careful planning and the development of coping thoughts that are tailored to particular anger triggers and distortions.

You can use what you've learned about anger distortions in the previous chapter to dramatically change your thinking when provoked. The key is to identify which anger distortion a particular trigger thought derives from, then use the countermeasures appropriate for that distortion to generate more realistic thinking. Here's a quick refresher of the countermeasures you might use to rewrite trigger thoughts sparked by the following distortions.

Magnifying/Catastrophizing. (1) Be realistically negative (e.g., it's disappointing or frustrating, not terrible or awful). Ask, "How bad is it really?," then answer honestly. (2) Use very accurate language. (3) Look at the whole picture. Try to find evidence that the opposite is also true.

Overgeneralization. (1) Avoid general terms like "always," "all," and "every." (2) Use specific and accurate descriptions. (3) Look for exceptions to the rule. Recall how people sometimes act contrary to their tendencies.

Demanding/commanding. (1) People rarely do what they should do, only what they need or want to do. (2) Stay with your wants, desires, and preferences—not shoulds. Think, "I prefer," not "You ought to."

Inflammatory/global Labeling. (1) Be specific: focus on behavior, not the person as a whole.

Misattribution/Single Explanations. (1) Check out your assumptions about other people's motives.

(2) Find alternative explanations for the problem behavior.

Blaming. (1) Make a coping plan to solve the problem yourself. (2) Recognize that people are mostly doing the best they can—what they think will best meet their needs.

Each of the above countermeasures is a guideline to help you revise trigger thoughts. Here are some examples of how to use the suggested countermeasures to develop less angry thinking:

1. **Situation:** Your mother-in-law invites you to dinner, but cooks a dish you're allergic to.

    Trigger thought: This is her typical crap—I'm total chopped liver to her, I never count. The only thing she cares about is her precious daughter.

    Anger distortion: Overgeneralization (total chopped liver, I never count). Misattribution/single explanations (she cooked this because she doesn't care about me).

    Counterresponse plan: For overgeneralization, look for exceptions. For misattributions, look for alternative explanations.

Revised trigger thought: She cooked eggplant today, but it's also true she paid for my watercolor workshop and came over and made soup when I had the flu. She's seventy-five, so it may just be that she forgets.

2. **Situation:** Your husband is yelling at your daughter over not bringing an assignment home from school.

Trigger thoughts: He's doing damage. This is going to ruin their relationship. He's crazy.

Anger distortions: Magnifying/catastrophizing (he's doing damage, this will ruin their relationship). Inflammatory/global labeling (he's crazy).

Counterresponse plan: For magnifying/catastrophizing, be accurate and look at the whole picture. For inflammatory/global labeling, focus on specific behavior, not the person as a whole.

Revised trigger thought: He raises his voice maybe once a week, but most times they get through the homework okay. They even laugh a little. He doesn't hit her, he doesn't call her names. It's not crazy, it's just a bit loud and unsettling.

3. **Situation:** A male work colleague, who has sometimes been critical in the past, tells you that, "Women are not as committed to their careers as men."

Trigger thoughts: Stupid jerk! He shouldn't open his mouth when he doesn't know what he's talking about. He says this kind of sh– to annoy me.

Anger distortions: Inflammatory/global labeling (stupid jerk). Demanding/commanding (shouldn't open his mouth if he doesn't know what he's talking about). Misattribution/single explanations (says this to annoy me).

Counterresponse plan: For inflammatory/global labeling, focus on specific behavior, not the person as a whole. For demanding/commanding, remember that people do what they need to do, not what I want. For misattribution/single explanations, find an alternative explanation.

Revised trigger thought: He makes ignorant remarks about women at times. I suspect he needs to do it because he feels very insecure and copes by putting women down. These comments may be a way to manage his poor self-esteem.

The next two examples will require a little thought on your part. After you've read through the situation and trigger thoughts, try to identify the key anger distortions and a counterresponse plan for each of them. An answer key is provided at the end.

4. **Situation:** Your neighbor keeps blocking your driveway with his garbage can.

    Trigger thoughts: That f—ing idiot is making me late for work. He always does that.

    Anger distortions: (hint—there are three anger distortions)

    [Space Left Intentionally Blank in the Original Source]

    Counterresponse plan:

    [Space Left Intentionally Blank in the Original Source]

    Revised trigger thoughts: Okay, the blind old coot got the can in my way. This is only the fourth time in six months, and it takes me exactly two minutes to pull it out of the way. I'll check the driveway before I get in the car. That'll make it easier.

5. **Situation:** Your roommate hasn't fed her dog or bird; the bird is screeching and the dog is constantly jumping on you when you come in from work.

    Trigger thoughts: I can't stand this ... this is too much, this is totally f—ed up. She's ruining my evening; she shouldn't have pets.

    Anger distortions: (hint—there are four anger distortions)

    [Space Left Intentionally Blank in the Original Source]

    Counterresponse Plan:

    [Space Left Intentionally Blank in the Original Source]

    Revised trigger thought: She forgets a few times a week. This is a brief, unpleasant moment till I feed them, but it's nothing horrible. She's scattered and forgetful. I'd prefer she remembered, but she's doing her best.

Answer Key

Example 4:

Anger distortions: inflammatory/global labeling (f—ing idiot), blaming (making me late for work), overgeneralization (he always does that)

Counterresponse plan: For inflammatory/global labeling, make a funny label. For blaming, make a problem-solving plan. For overgeneralization, be accurate.

Example 5:

Anger distortions: magnifying/catastrophizing (can't stand this; this is too much), inflammatory/global labeling (totally f—-ed up), blaming (she's ruining my evening), demanding/commanding (she shouldn't have pets)

Counterresponse plan: For magnifying/catastrophizing, be realistically negative. For inflammatory/global labeling, focus on specific behavior. For blaming, recognize that she's doing the best she can. For demanding/commanding, stay with desires and preferences.

Creating Coping Thoughts

This is your chance to develop revised trigger thoughts for some of your own anger situations. Complete the Creating Coping Thoughts Worksheet for an anger situation recorded in your most recent Anger Log.

CREATING COPING THOUGHTS—Worksheet

Complete the following for each significant trigger thought in an anger situation from your most recent Anger Log:

1. Trigger thoughts that inflame my anger:

a.

b.

c.

2. Anger distortions that underlie my trigger thoughts:

a.

b.

c.

3. Counterresponse plan for each of my trigger thoughts (e.g., looking for exceptions, alternative explanations, preferences not shoulds, and so on).

Revised trigger thought based on each counterresponse plan.

a. Counterresponse plan:

Revised trigger thought:

b. Counterresponse plan:

Revised trigger thought:

c. Counterresponse plan:

Revised trigger thought:

4. Helpful coping thoughts (see General Coping Thoughts List earlier in this chapter):

a.

b.

c.

To give you an idea of how the worksheet can be used, an example follows from a forty-five-year-old customer service rep. She finds herself getting angry at customers who are themselves upset about delayed or mishandled orders.

1. Trigger   thoughts that inflame my anger:

   a. I can't stand this.

   b. They use me as a punching bag because I can't fight back.

   c. Just an endless string of crazy people.

2. Anger distortions that underlie my trigger thoughts:

   a. Magnifying.

   b. Misattributions/single explanations.

   c. Overgeneralization and inflammatory/global labeling.

3. Counterresponse plan for each of my trigger thoughts:

   a. Counterresponse plan: Be accurate, look at the whole picture.

   Revised trigger thoughts: It's not that bad—usually only one customer in ten is really obnoxious.

   b. Counterresponse plan: Alternative explanations

Revised trigger thoughts: They're frustrated and, I think, afraid they'll be screwed somehow.

c. Counterresponse plan: Be specific and accurate.

Revised trigger thought: It's 10 percent rude people and 90 percent nice ones.

4. Helpful coping thoughts:

    a. Just as long as I keep my cool, I'm in control.

    b. Take a deep breath and relax.

    c. Let them get all upset, I can stay calm.

Homework

There are four specific things you'll need to do over the next seven to ten days to strengthen the anger management skills you've learned so far:

1. Use one of your three general coping thoughts whenever you find yourself responding with anger.

2. Practice cue-controlled relaxation whenever you feel stressed or the beginnings of anger. Also continue to practice all three key relaxation skills and record the dates in your Relaxation Log.

3.   Continue to note in your Anger Log all significant anger situations.

4.   Use your Creating Coping Thoughts Worksheet to develop revised trigger thoughts for any significant anger situation recorded in your log. There are four extra worksheets at the end of this chapter. (Image 8.1, 8.2)

Anger Log II

Provocative Situation	The Screen	Anger Rating 0–100	Behavior	Outcomes -10 to +10	
Sensory Input (Objective data from what you hear, see, and touch)	(Your conclusions, assumptions, interpretations, beliefs, and trigger thoughts)			Self	Others

Image 8.1

Relaxation Log II

Date	Relaxation Imagery	Cue-Controlled Relaxation	Relaxation without Tension

Image 8.2: INSTRUCTIONS: Put a check mark under the relaxation exercises completed on each date.

CREATING COPING THOUGHTS—Worksheet

Complete the following for each significant trigger thought in an anger situation.

1. Trigger thoughts that inflame my anger:

a.

b.

c.

2. Anger distortions that underlie my trigger thoughts:

a.

b.

c.

3. Counterresponse plan for each of my trigger thoughts (e.g., looking for exceptions, alternative explanations, preferences instead of shoulds, etc.). Revised trigger thought based on each counterresponse plan.

a. Counterresponse plan:

Revised trigger thought:

b. Counterresponse plan:

Revised trigger thought:

c. Counterresponse plan:

Revised trigger thought:

4. Helpful coping thoughts (see General Coping Thoughts List earlier in this chapter):

a.

b.

c.

CHAPTER 9

ANGER INOCULATION I

This chapter will begin to teach you a new set of coping skills and help you to keep track of which coping strategies work best for you during provocative situations. It's important to remember to use the relaxation skills that you've already mastered. Deep breathing, cue-controlled relaxation, and relaxation without tension (focused on one particularly tense area only) are all very helpful in provocative situations.

Second, remember to use the new coping thoughts you learned in the last chapter during provocative situations. Have a few key coping thoughts written down. Carry them with you and review them every day, to better keep them in mind. It's also good to keep in mind that behavioral coping strategies are available. During a provocative situation, you can reduce tension by lowering your voice, looking for a compromise, or agreeing to talk about it later. Finally, remember that you are not stuck. It's perfectly okay to simply leave a provocative situation if you see that you're on the slippery slope to an anger disaster.

How to Monitor Your Coping Efforts

We have developed a useful tool for you to keep track of all your coping strategies and their relative effectiveness. You will find a blank copy of Anger Log III on the next page. As you can see, there are several columns, providing spaces to list provocative situations and their associated anger ratings. There are also columns for listing coping strategies and outcomes.

Beginning with the provocative situation on the left side of the page, you can see that it's broken down into two parts. First, under Sensory Input, write down the actual objective data that you are aware of. This should include the things that you actually can hear, see, or touch. Next, under the heading, The Screen, we want you to write down your interpretations of the data. This would include assumptions, conclusions, beliefs, and trigger thoughts. To the right of that is a column for making an initial, baseline rating of your experience of anger associated with this situation. Use a rating scale of 0 to 100, with 0 being no anger at all, and 100 being absolute, total rage.

Now move your attention to the next column to the right. This is where we want you to write down the coping strategies (if any) that you tried in response to the provocative situation. Then rate the amount of anger experienced after your coping efforts. Use the same 0- to 100-point scale as before. By comparing these ratings to the baseline, you can assess how well your coping strategies have worked in this situation. (Image 9.1, 9.2)

Anger Log III

Provocative Situation Sensory Input (Objective data from what you hear, see, and touch)	The Screen (Your conclusions, assumptions, interpretations, beliefs, and trigger thoughts)	Anger Rating 0–100	Coping Strategies Breathing, relaxation, coping thoughts, coping behaviors.	Anger Rating 0–100	Outcomes Rating -10 to +10 Self Others	

Image 9.1

Anger Log III

Provocative Situation — Sensory Input (Objective data from what you hear, see, and touch)	The Screen (Your conclusions, assumptions, interpretations, beliefs, and trigger thoughts)	Anger Rating 0–100	Coping Strategies — Breathing, relaxation, coping thoughts, coping behaviors.	Anger Rating 0–100	Outcomes Rating -10 to +10 Self	Others
A car swoops in front of me on the high-way. I hit the brakes hard. Squealing sound. Hands clenched on wheel.	He did that on purpose because he wants to scare me. F–king a–hole?	40	Deep breathing, relax without tension, focus on hands. "It's not directed at me." "He's just out for a thrill"	5	+7	0
Teenager's room. A complete mess. Home-work not done. Talk-ing to friend on telephone.	She has absolutely no respect for me. I've told her a thousand times and she never listens.	50	Deep breathing, relaxation imagery. "She's just being a teenager." "I was the same way at her age."	20	+3	+2
Doctor's receptionist calls, canceling my appointment.	He doesn't give a damn about any of his patients.	60	No coping	60	-6	0

Image 9.2

Finally, use the columns to the far right to evaluate the outcome of your anger in conjunction with any coping efforts. Negative numbers would indicate an unfavorable result, while positive numbers indicate a favorable outcome. By rating the outcomes for both yourself and others, you can see how your anger and your coping strategies have differential effects.

In order to help you with this process, we've included a completed sample log with three anger situations, following the blank log.

Anger Inoculation

Now it's time to learn more about a process known as *anger inoculation.* Don't worry—it has nothing to do with needles! Essentially, anger inoculation is similar to the more familiar technique called stress inoculation, but specifically designed to deal with anger. Anger inoculation is basically a structured rehearsal of your coping thoughts and relaxation coping skills. You simply practice your new coping skills in response to imagined anger scenes. Here's the basic sequence:

1. Create 2 mild to moderate (40–50 SUDS) anger scenes. Incidentally, SUDS stands for Subjective Units of Distress. You can create your own unique SUDS scale by assigning points to various situa-

tions, from 0 (none) to 100 (absolutely unbearable).

2. Next, identify the trigger thoughts and anger distortions in each scene.

3. Using the Creating Coping Thoughts Worksheet later in this chapter, develop two or three coping thoughts for each scene.

4. Then, relax using whichever brief method works best for you. Try relaxation imagery, cue-controlled relaxation, and perhaps relaxation without tension.

5. Once you feel relaxed, start to visualize the first mild to moderate anger scene. See all the detail, hear what's being said, and notice your feelings and any bodily sensations. Crank up your anger with a few juicy trigger thoughts. Stay with it. Allow the anger to intensify as much as possible. Maintain the scene for thirty seconds.

6. Then, mentally erase the scene and begin relaxation imagery, cue-controlled relaxation, and perhaps relaxation without tension (focused on a particular muscle area). Also rehearse two or three coping thoughts until you feel completely calm again.

7.   Repeat the entire sequence again, using the second anger scene.

8.   Keep alternating the two scenes for four to six repetitions of each.

Right now you should create the two mild to moderate (40–50 SUDS) anger scenes that you will use to practice anger inoculation. This technique works best when the images in the scene are clear and strong. That's why it's necessary to get as much detail into the scene as possible. The scene should be something that has really happened, and is fresh enough to easily recall. To develop a scene fully, start by closing your eyes. Mentally look around and notice the environment. What time of day is it? Be aware of the temperature. Listen to the sounds around you. What are people saying? Notice feelings inside your body. Is there a tingling or tense sensation somewhere in your body? Are there any smells? Use the following Creating Anger Scenes Worksheets to write down your notes.

We've also provided a sample worksheet with two examples, filled out by Suzy, a young woman with an overly protective uncle and a less-than-perfect boyfriend.

CREATING ANGER SCENES—Worksheet

Mild-to-Moderate (40–50 SUDS) Anger Scenes

Instructions: In the spaces provided below, fill in the details of two situations in which you would experience mild-to-moderate anger. Include details about the physical environment and what other people are saying and doing. Also describe your own trigger thoughts, feelings, and physiological reactions.

Mild-to-Moderate Anger Situation 1:

[Space Left Intentionally Blank in the Original Source]

Mild-to-Moderate Anger Situation 2:

[Space Left Intentionally Blank in the Original Source]

CREATING ANGER SCENES—Examples

Mild-to-Moderate (40–50 SUDS) Anger Scenes

Instructions: In the spaces provided below, fill in the details of two situations in which you would experience mild-to-moderate anger. Include details about the physical environment and what other people are saying and doing. Also describe your own trigger thoughts, feelings, and physiological reactions.

Mild-to-Moderate Anger Situation 1:

I'm on my way to meet Uncle Willy for lunch. And I'm already feeling a knot in my stomach. I know that he's going to say something judgmental. Warm day, outside café. Uncle Willy waves me over to the table, but his face looks serious. Even before the waiter comes to take our order, Uncle Willy says, "I want to talk to you about your boyfriend. I don't know why you put up with him. He's not good enough for you. He has that stupid pizza job and I think that he's taking advantage of you." I think, "There you go again. Always putting me down and trying to run my life." I sit there and seethe for the rest of the lunch. I can't get what he said out of my mind.

Mild-to-Moderate Anger Situation 2:

Here's Randy, on time for dinner but never on time for anything else. "You know, Randy, I like having dinner with you, and I don't mind cooking for you. But I wish that you would contribute in some way.

> *Maybe bring flowers or a bottle of wine." My neck starts to tense up, but I continue anyway. "And you never even offer to help with the cleanup or the dishes. I'm sick and tired of feeling unappreciated." Then Randy goes, "Take a chill pill, you're always kicking my ass about something. Your problem is you don't know how to enjoy yourself." Then I think to myself that maybe Uncle Willy was right.*

The next step is to identify some trigger thoughts and anger distortions associated with the scene. Visualize each scene you've created and notice what you're thinking. Once the trigger thoughts become clear, try to link them to the appropriate anger distortion. With this in mind, we want you to fill out a Creating Coping Thoughts Worksheet for each anger scene that you created. There are two blank worksheets on the following pages.

To give you an example of how the worksheet looks, we've enclosed a sample filled out by Tom, a fifty-three-year-old middle manager working in a large printing firm. He keeps finding himself getting angry at some younger employees whom he considers unmotivated.

Now, let's follow along as Tom goes through the anger inoculation sequence:

First, he begins the relaxation process by doing some deep breathing. Then he closes his eyes and calls up his relaxation image, which for him is a deserted beach on the island of Molokai. He can feel the gentle breeze and warm sun, and he can hear waves lapping up on shore. He does some cue-controlled relaxation, feeling himself let go completely.

Then, he switches to the mild-to-moderate anger scene. He comes to work and the first thing he notices is a couple of the younger employees hanging around the coffee room. They should be working. When they see him, they stop talking and Tom thinks he sees one of them hide a smirk. Tom feels a knot in his stomach as they saunter off without saying a word. Tom's trigger thoughts: "Lazy ... self-centered ... deadwood like that is running the company." [Thirty seconds go by quickly.]

Now, he mentally erases the anger scene. He pictures a slow fade-out like in a movie he once saw. He tries to get back to the beach on Molokai, but it won't come. A few deep breaths and he switches to cue-controlled relaxation. Then relaxation without tension focused on the knot in his stomach. That's it. He's feeling more relaxed. Now he rehearses two of his favorite coping thoughts. "Just take a deep breath and relax"; "I'm in control, just keep cool." After several minutes, he feels completely calm again.

Switching to his second scene, Tom imagines that it's lunchtime at the plant. As he's leaving for lunch, he sees the two young employees leaving the boss's office. They see him, whisper something to each other, and walk off in the other direction. He's sure that they've just been bad-mouthing him to his boss. Trigger thoughts: "They're in there sucking up. Probably covering their asses by blaming others for not getting the work done." Tom holds a mental picture of the scene for thirty seconds.

Scene does slow fade-out. And Tom focuses on his stomach, relaxation without tension. That's it, just let go. Now some deep breathing with his cue word, and here comes the beach on Molokai. All right. Now some coping thoughts: "I can stay calm, I'm in control." "Their work habits don't affect me." Within a short while Tom feels completely calm again, and thinks to himself, "Yes. This is really working."

Tom keeps alternating the two scenes for a repetition of five times each.

Homework

1. Develop two anger scenes and practice four to six repetitions of each scene, on two separate occasions, before moving on to the next chapter.

2. Keep practicing relaxation and keep up the notations in the Relaxation Log.

3. Keep your record of anger events using Anger Log III.

We know that this chapter makes a lot of demands on your time and energy. But it's worth it to minimize the devastating effects anger can have on you and your loved ones. The stronger your commitment to this healing process, the better your life will feel.

CREATING COPING THOUGHTS—Worksheet

Complete the following for each significant trigger thought in an anger situation.

1. Trigger thoughts that inflame my anger:

a.

b.

c.

2. Anger distortions that underlie my trigger thoughts:

a.

b.

c.

3. Counterresponse plan for each of my trigger thoughts (e.g., looking for exceptions, alternative explanations, preferences instead of shoulds, etc.). Revised trigger thought based on each counterresponse plan.

a. Counterresponse plan:

Revised trigger thought:

b. Counterresponse plan:

Revised trigger thought:

c. Counterresponse plan:

Revised trigger thought:

4. Helpful coping thoughts (see General Coping Thoughts List earlier in this chapter):

a.

b.

---

c.

CREATING COPING THOUGHTS—Worksheet

Complete the following for each significant trigger thought in an anger situation.

1. Trigger thoughts that inflame my anger:

a.

b.

c.

2. Anger distortions that underlie my trigger thoughts:

a.

b.

c.

3. Counterresponse plan for each of my trigger thoughts (e.g., looking for exceptions, alternative explanations, preferences instead of shoulds, etc.).

Revised trigger thought based on each counterresponse plan.

a. Counterresponse plan:

Revised trigger thought:

b. Counterresponse plan:

Revised trigger thought:

c. Counterresponse plan:

Revised trigger thought:

4. Helpful coping thoughts (see General Coping Thoughts List earlier in this chapter):

a.

b.

c.

CREATING COPING THOUGHTS—Example

Complete the following for each significant trigger thought in an anger situation.

1. Trigger thoughts that inflame my anger:

a. *Lazy ... self-centered ... deadwood*

b. They're ruining this company.

c.

2. Anger distortions that underlie my trigger thoughts:

a. *Global labeling*

b. *Magnifying*

c.

3. Counterresponse plan for each of my trigger thoughts (e.g., looking for exceptions, alternative explanations, preferences instead of shoulds, etc.). Revised trigger thought based on each counterresponse plan.

a. Counterresponse plan: *Accurate statements, no put-down labels*

Revised trigger thought: *They're taking more frequent breaks than they should, but their work habits don't affect me.*

b. Counterresponse plan: *Be accurate and specific.*

Revised trigger thought: *They're wasting 5 to 10 minutes, that's all. That will have zero impact on a big company like this.*

c. Counterresponse plan:

Revised trigger thought:

4. Helpful coping thoughts (see General Coping Thoughts List earlier in this chapter): (Image 9.3, 9.4)

a. *Just take a deep breath and relax.*

b. *I'm in control, just keep cool.*

c.

Anger Log III

Provocative Situation Sensory Input (Objective data from what you hear, see, and touch)	The Screen (Your conclusions, assumptions, interpretations, beliefs, and trigger thoughts)	Anger Rating 0–100	Coping Strategies Breathing, relaxation, coping thoughts, coping behaviors.	Anger Rating 0–100	Outcomes Rating -10 to +10 Self — Others

Image 9.3

Relaxation Log II

Date	Relaxation Imagery	Cue-Controlled Relaxation	Relaxation without Tension

Image 9.4: INSTRUCTIONS: Put a check mark under the relaxation exercises completed on each date.

CHAPTER 10

ANGER INOCULATION II

Before moving on to this next level, take a moment to look at and evaluate the results from your most recent entries in Anger Log III. Have you begun to cope with provocative situations as they arise? If so, what coping strategies are working best for you? In the space provided below, write in anything that's worked well for each category:

1. Relaxation Coping:

    [Space Left Intentionally Blank in the Original Source]

2. Coping Thoughts:

    [Space Left Intentionally Blank in the Original Source]

3. Coping Behaviors:

    [Space Left Intentionally Blank in the Original Source]

Anger Inoculation—Moderate Anger Scenes

Now it's time to start practicing anger inoculation with two moderate (50–60 SUDS) anger scenes. Just like last time, we want you to imagine an anger-producing scene and then manage the anger by using relaxation and coping thoughts.

It's really important to try hard to make these anger scenes as vivid as possible. That means including lots of specifics: what you see and hear, even smells associated with the scene, and also kinesthetic aspects like temperature and texture. It's also good to include details about emotional and physical reactions that are occurring during each scene. If you've been practicing all along, this will get easier and easier to accomplish over time.

Next, identify the trigger thoughts and anger distortions in each scene. These are important to include in your visualization because they crank up your anger. Now, using the Creating Anger Scenes Worksheet on the next page, write out two moderate anger scenes. In order to give you an idea of what this should look like, we've provided a sample worksheet with two examples.

When you feel completely prepared, you can go to a quiet, comfortable place and start the relaxation process. It usually works best to begin with relaxation imagery, then make a segue into cue-controlled relaxation, and perhaps relaxation without tension.

Once you feel relaxed, you can start the moderate anger scene, like pushing the PLAY button on your VCR remote control. Allow the anger to intensify by focusing on the images and trigger thoughts that really outrage you. Stay in the scene for thirty seconds.

Now erase the scene, like pushing the STOP button on the VCR remote, and then go back to the relaxation process again. Be sure, at the very least, to use cue-controlled relaxation. As you feel yourself begin to relax physically, repeat some of your coping thoughts. Continue until you feel completely calm.

Repeat the entire sequence again using the second anger scene. Keep alternating the two scenes for four to six repetitions of each. In a day or two, do the entire series (four to six alternating repetitions of each scene) once more.

By way of example, let's follow Jenny, a fifty-two-year-old divorced accountant, as she goes through the process with a moderate anger scene.

She begins relaxing by picturing herself in a childhood summer cabin in the Catskill Mountains. A gentle breeze is coming off the lake, and some birds are chirping. She can smell her mother's apple pie cooling in the kitchen.

Now the scene shifts dramatically. It's a retirement "home," where the harsh odor of antiseptics doesn't quite mask the sweet, sickly, "old people" smell in the air. Jenny is coming to visit her mother, her heels clicking on the nearly empty hallway. "Why is it always me who has to take care of Mom? My brothers and sisters never help at all." Her stomach starts to tighten as she nears the room. Open door, "Hi Mom." "Oh, it's you, finally. Nobody ever comes to see me. I guess it's 'cause I'm not cooking. After everything I did for you I think you could at least show up here once in a while." Jenny thinks, "I can't stand this for even one second more."

After thirty seconds, CLICK, mercifully the scene ends and Jenny is back in the Catskills. Cue-controlled relaxation, and Jenny thinks, "My brothers and sisters are doing the best they can, they have kids of their own to take care of." "I'll only stay for fifteen minutes—my mother deserves that much." After a few minutes, she feels calm again.

Now a new scene begins to take shape. Jenny is at the supermarket. It's crowded at this time of day.

Feeling good about getting the last shopping cart, she starts to smile. This quickly turns into a grimace as she realizes that it has a bad wheel, veering to the left with a constant squeaking noise. Her hands tighten on the cart's handle. Finally, finished shopping, she gets on line at the checkout counter. The line moves along fairly quickly until the last person ahead of her starts having an argument with the clerk. "This was on sale, three for a dollar." The clerk calls for an assistant to go check out the price.

All the other lines are moving nicely except this one. "This always happens to me. At this rate I'll miss the evening news on TV." Assistant returns, the customer was mistaken. Now she's fumbling through her purse looking for discount coupons. Finally, giving up, she says, "Okay, I'll write you a check." When the clerk asks for ID she doesn't have any. The clerk calls for a manager. Jenny's stomach is tightening up. Minutes go by. Nothing happens. The clerk calls again for a manager. "Oh, come on! What a god-damned idiot!"

CREATING ANGER SCENES—Worksheet

Moderate (50–60 SUDS) Anger Scenes

Instructions: In the spaces provided below, fill in the details of two situations in which you would experience moderate anger. Include details about the physical environment and what other people are saying and doing. Also describe your own trigger thoughts, feelings, and physiological reactions.

Moderate Anger Situation 1:

[Space Left Intentionally Blank in the Original Source]

Moderate Anger Situation 2:

[Space Left Intentionally Blank in the Original Source]

CREATING ANGER SCENES—Examples

Moderate (50–60 SUDS) Anger Scenes

Instructions: In the spaces provided below, fill in the details of two situations in which you would experience moderate anger. Include details about the physical environment and what other people are saying and doing. Also describe your own trigger thoughts, feelings, and physiological reactions.

Moderate Anger Situation 1:

Last weekend I decided it's time to do my laundry. Finally got all the dirty, smelly clothes into a large garbage bag. I'm walking to the Laundromat when it starts to pour. I'm hurrying, but have to stop at a red light. A car speeds around the corner, nearly hitting me, and splashing my shoes. I feel my body go tense. I get to the Laundromat. There's only one empty washing machine and I run to get it, putting my coins in the slot, and jamming them home. Then I notice a small sign saying it's out of order. I push the coin return button and nothing happens. I kick the side of the washer and say, "Damn machine." I feel a surge of anger.

Moderate Anger Situation 2:

It's Friday evening. I finally get home after an hour and a half on the road. I feel tired and uptight, just wanting to relax and be taken care of. My wannabe writer husband comes out of his "den," unshaven and looking sheepish. "I haven't had time to go shopping. I've been too busy with this new poem." My neck gets tense. I snap out, "Thanks a lot," and go into the living room. The morning news paper is still strewn all over the place. "Do I have to do everything myself?" I mumble under my breath through clenched teeth. I feel my anger start to rise. I go into the kitchen and find the dirty dishes still in the sink. "You're useless, Bob," I shout as my husband enters the room.

CREATING COPING THOUGHTS—Worksheet

Complete the following for each significant trigger thought in an anger situation.

1. Trigger thoughts that inflame my anger:

a.

b.

c.

2. Anger distortions that underlie my trigger thoughts:

a.

b.

c.

3. Counterresponse plan for each of my trigger thoughts (e.g., looking for exceptions, alternative explanations, preferences instead of shoulds, etc.).

Revised trigger thought based on each counterresponse plan.

a. Counterresponse plan:

Revised trigger thought:

b. Counterresponse plan:

Revised trigger thought:

c. Counterresponse plan:

Revised trigger thought:

4. Helpful coping thoughts (see General Coping Thoughts List earlier in this chapter):

a.

b.

c.

CREATING COPING THOUGHTS—Worksheet

Complete the following for each significant trigger thought in an anger situation.

1. Trigger thoughts that inflame my anger:

a.

b.

c.

2. Anger distortions that underlie my trigger thoughts:

a.

b.

c.

3. Counterresponse plan for each of my trigger thoughts (e.g., looking for exceptions, alternative explanations, preferences instead of shoulds, etc.). Revised trigger thought based on each counterresponse plan.

a. Counterresponse plan:

Revised trigger thought:

b. Counterresponse plan:

Revised trigger thought:

c. Counterresponse plan:

Revised trigger thought:

4. Helpful coping thoughts (see General Coping Thoughts List earlier in this chapter):

a.

b.

c.

CLICK, back in the Catskills, a sunny afternoon. "It's okay, they're doing the best they can." "So what if I miss the news. It'll be in the paper tomorrow anyway." Cue-controlled relaxation, relaxation without tension focusing on her stomach, more coping thoughts, more relaxation, and eventually calm.

Jenny alternates the two scenes—anger at her mother, and then anger at the supermarket lady—for four to six repetitions each.

Anger Inoculation—New Format

When you feel comfortable managing moderate anger scenes, it's time to move up a notch to moderate-to-high (60–75 SUDS) anger. This time, however, you will not be erasing the scene as before. We want you to continue visualizing the provocative scene while *simultaneously* using a variety of coping strategies to reduce the anger. In other words, you'll cope with your anger *in* the scene, not after it.

Begin by creating two moderate-to-high anger scenes, using lots of detail, and write them out on the Creating Anger Scenes Worksheet provided on the next page. Next, identify the trigger thoughts and anger distortions in each scene. Then, develop coping thoughts for each scene, recording all of the information on the Creating Coping Thoughts Worksheets provided. Once you've finished all the preparatory work, relax and start to visualize the first scene. *Note:* Don't start any coping strategies until the scene is fully developed

Now, here's the important part: We want you to maintain the image of the provocation, while at the same time practicing your coping skills. Hold on to the image while using cue-controlled relaxation, and perhaps releasing tension in a tight area of your body. Continue to stay locked on to the image, and use one or two coping thoughts. Then go back to cue-controlled relaxation, more coping thoughts, etc. It's not easy to do several things at the same time. But, with practice, you will be able to balance the visualization with the coping strategies. Only when you feel completely calm in the anger scene should you erase it and take a break using relaxation imagery.

As an example, we can follow along as Jim, a forty-two-year-old, married, freelance building contractor with two kids, works his way through the moderate-to-high anger scene that he's created. He's already prepared himself by identifying trigger thoughts, anger distortions, and the appropriate countermeasures. Now he goes to his den, closes his eyes, and begins to relax by visualizing a meadow in Yosemite National Park. Deep breath. Filtered sunlight, shadows float across the meadow, a doe and a fawn shyly step out of the forest. Cue-controlled relaxation.

CLICK. Now to work. Jim is riding in his old pickup truck, bouncing along as his worn-out shocks make a creaking noise. His hands tense on the steering wheel as he hits a pothole. "Damn, I need a new truck, but I can't afford it." Cell phone rings. It's Carstairs, complaining that the crew that was supposed to be putting in the new roof hasn't shown up yet, and it's nearly noon. "Shit, I can't afford to mess up on this job too. Everybody is complaining about something, and I'm not getting any new referrals." He thinks to himself, "That's what I get for using cheap labor—those guys are just plain lazy and don't want to work. They're all worthless pieces of crap."

With this scene firmly established, and feeling quite angry as he relives it, Jim is ready to start coping. Cue-controlled relaxation, that's better. Coping thoughts: "My job is solving problems. That's what I do. No big deal. Breathe and relax. I can handle it." Jim focuses on relaxing his stomach, which is tight, letting each deep breath loosen the knot. More coping thoughts, more cue-controlled relaxation until his whole body seems to have let go and he feels calm again.

CREATING ANGER SCENES—Worksheet

Moderate-to-High (60–75 SUDS) Anger Scenes

Instructions: In the spaces provided below, fill in the details of two situations in which you would experience moderate-to-high anger. Include details about the physical environment and what other people are saying and doing. Also describe your own trigger thoughts, feelings, and physiological reactions.

Moderate-to-High Anger Situation 1:

[Space Left Intentionally Blank in the Original Source]

Moderate-to-High Anger Situation 2:

[Space Left Intentionally Blank in the Original Source]

CREATING COPING THOUGHTS—Worksheet

Complete the following for each significant trigger thought in an anger situation.

1. Trigger thoughts that inflame my anger:

a.

b.

c.

2. Anger distortions that underlie my trigger thoughts:

a.

b.

c.

3. Counterresponse plan for each of my trigger thoughts (e.g., looking for exceptions, alternative explanations, preferences instead of shoulds, etc.). Revised trigger thought based on each counterresponse plan.

a. Counterresponse plan:

Revised trigger thought:

b. Counterresponse plan:

Revised trigger thought:

c. Counterresponse plan:

Revised trigger thought:

4. Helpful coping thoughts (see General Coping Thoughts List earlier in this chapter):

a.

b.

c.

CREATING COPING THOUGHTS—Worksheet

Complete the following for each significant trigger thought in an anger situation.

1. Trigger thoughts that inflame my anger:

a.

b.

c.

2. Anger distortions that underlie my trigger thoughts:

a.

b.

c.

3. Counterresponse plan for each of my trigger thoughts (e.g., looking for exceptions, alternative explanations, preferences instead of shoulds, etc.).

Revised trigger thought based on each counterresponse plan.

a. Counterresponse plan:

Revised trigger thought:

b. Counterresponse plan:

Revised trigger thought:

c. Counterresponse plan:

Revised trigger thought:

4. Helpful coping thoughts (see General Coping Thoughts List earlier in this chapter):

a.

b.

c.

Only when the anger is completely gone does he click off the scene. Now he returns to the relaxation imagery of the Yosemite meadow.

Now Jim switches to his second moderate-to-high anger scene.

Jim comes home at seven P.M., exhausted. His wife Shirley meets him at the door and says, "I've had it with your son. He won't clean his room. You deal with him." Jim stomps to Chad's room, which looks like a cyclone hit it. He can smell the remains of half-eaten pizza, and sees pizza cartons and empty soda cans strewn all over. His son is lying on an unmade bed chatting on the telephone, while MTV blares on the TV. "Hang up that phone son, we need to talk." Chad replies, "Oh man, can't you see I'm busy?" Jim feels himself get cold all over. His right arm tenses as his hand forms a fist. "Get off that damn phone and clean up this room right now." Chad, not really paying attention, says, "All right, Dad, I'll do it later." With a snarl, Jim grabs the receiver and hangs up the phone. "Do it now, or get out of my house," he yells.

Still quivering with anger, and attention locked on the scene, Jim begins to use his coping strategies. First, cue-controlled relaxation, then coping thoughts. "I'm still in control. Keep cool now." Relaxation without tension focused on his forearm, biceps, and fist. "He's just a kid, go easy on him." Deep breathing. Slowly, a sense of calm returns.

Only after the anger is completely gone does he click back to the relaxation image in Yosemite.

Jim switches back and forth between each scene four to six times. Within a day or two, he does the entire series (four to six alternating repetitions of each scene) once more.

Homework

1. Continue to track your anger experiences and coping efforts using Anger Log III.

2. Continue to practice cue-controlled relaxation whenever stressed, and notice how much easier it's getting to relax whenever you put your mind to it. Practice all three key relaxation skills and note the details in the Relaxation Log.

3. Use the Creating Coping Thoughts Worksheet for any provocative situation where you couldn't manage your trigger thoughts or control your anger.

4. Make sure you've completed two entire series (four to six alternating repetitions of each scene) for both the moderate and moderate-to-high anger level scenes. (Image 10.1, 10.2)

Anger Log III

Provocative Situation Sensory Input (Objective data from what you hear, see, and touch)	The Screen (Your conclusions, assumptions, interpretations, beliefs, and trigger thoughts)	Anger Rating 0–100	Coping Strategies Breathing, relaxation, coping thoughts, coping behaviors.	Anger Rating 0–100	Outcomes Rating -10 to +10 Self Others

Image 10.1

191

Date	Relaxation Imagery	Cue-Controlled Relaxation	Relaxation without Tension

Image 10.2: INSTRUCTIONS: Put a check mark under the relaxation exercises completed on each date.

CHAPTER 11

ANGER INOCULATION III

Before we move on to the highest levels of anger inoculation, it's useful to spend some time reviewing the information that has accumulated in your Anger Log III records. In particular, we want you to look back on times when you felt upset but somehow weren't able to mobilize and use your new skills.

On the checklist below, mark the categories of anger situations where you either forget to use your new skills, or they don't seem to work.

_ Anger with people you supervise.

_ Anger with authority figures.

_ Anger with spouse/partner/lover.

_ Anger with children.

_ Anger with close friends.

_ Anger with strangers (i.e., road rage, anger at store clerks, receptionists, etc.)

_ Anger with parents.

_ Anger when you feel criticized.

_ Anger when you feel disrespected.

_ Anger when you feel hurt.

_ Anger when you feel pressured to do something.

_ Anger when you feel humiliated/shamed.

_ Anger when you feel disappointed.

_ Anger when you feel frustrated.

_ Anger when you feel threatened.

_ Anger when you feel guilty or wrong.

_ Anger when you're scared something bad will happen.

_ Anger when you're tired/overwhelmed/pushed to the limit/running on empty.

_ Anger when people don't live up to your expectations.

_ Anger when people don't listen to you.

The categories you marked represent ongoing problems. Now, go back over the list and put a star next to the top three in terms of their impact on you. Then, for each of the starred categories, we want you to identify the following:

1. One strategy to remind you to use your coping skills.

2. An intervention point, i.e., the "red flag" behavior or step in the escalation process when you're going to do something different.

3. One (foolproof) coping response you're sure to use. This can be either a relaxation skill, a coping thought, or something you'd say or do differently.

Here are some examples:

One of the starred items on Maggie's list was "Anger with children"—specifically, her teenage daughter Ashley, who was an expert at pushing her buttons. Since many angry situations began in the kitchen, Maggie decided to use the refrigerator as a reminder site. She found a picture of an atomic bomb explosion and attached it to the door with magnets, as a subtle hint about going ballistic. Her red-flag behavior was when she started to sound like her own mother, hearing her voice get high and sharp. For a surefire coping response, Maggie chose cue-controlled relaxation, using the cue word "floating."

One of Bob's starred items was "Anger with people you supervise." He put a wood carving of an African warrior on his desk at work to remind him this *wasn't* a battle. For his intervention point, he chose to be aware of tapping his right foot and talking in a harsh, lecturing tone. Bob had noticed that when he felt annoyed at Lester, whom he supervised, he would start to tap his foot and talk as if Lester were stupid. He then chose the coping thought, "He's doing his best and I'm not going to mess with him," as his foolproof coping response.

There are three blank Target Problem Worksheets available at the end of this chapter. Fill out one for each of your identified target problems.

Anger Inoculation—High Anger Situations

Now it's time to move on to anger inoculation with high (75–85 SUDS) anger situations. Use the Creating Anger Scenes Worksheet on the next page to develop two scenes that are rich in detail. An example of a completed worksheet is also provided. Next, identify the trigger thoughts and anger distortions in the scene. Then, develop some appropriate coping thoughts and record them on the Creating Coping Thoughts Worksheets on the following pages.

CREATING ANGER SCENES—Worksheet

High (75–85 SUDS) Anger Scenes

Instructions: In the spaces provided below, fill in the details of two situations in which you would experience high levels of anger. Include details about the physical environment and what other people are saying and doing. Also describe your own trigger thoughts, feelings, and physiological reactions.

High Anger Situation 1:

[Space Left Intentionally Blank in the Original Source]

High Anger Situation 2:

[Space Left Intentionally Blank in the Original Source]

CREATING ANGER SCENES—Examples

High (75–85 SUDS) Anger Scenes

Instructions: In the spaces provided below, fill in the details of two situations in which you would experience high levels of anger. Include details about the physical environment and what other people are saying and doing. Also describe your own trigger thoughts, feelings, and physiological reactions.

High Anger Situation 1:

I'm sitting in my cold super's office thinking, "I'm a glorified janitor." People call me at all times of the day and night, expecting me to drop everything and fix this, fix that. Canfield, that looney tune in #15, calls to complain that I didn't clean up enough when I fixed his sink. He's an a—hole, like a lot of them in this building. Then Canfield says I should get a move on and clean under his sink right now or he's going to complain to the landlord. Stomach tense. I tell him to clean his own damn sink, and he says f—k you. Hands balled into fists. I've had it with his crazy shit. I'm only getting a lousy couple of hundred bucks for this. Treating me like dirt.

High Anger Situation 2:

Being a little league baseball coach. I'm sitting in the car sopping wet, driving half the players home from our rained-out ballgame. Most of the parents don't even show up for the games, and when they do, they're all over my ass about why their kid isn't batting cleanup. Stomach knots up. First, the damn kids don't want to practice, and then they throw a fit if I don't give them enough playing time. This kid Sal tells me to drop him off way the hell over at the Hillsdale mall. I tell him to forget it. He says maybe he'll quit the team then. I can feel how wet my clothes are, sticking to the seat. Flushed feeling in my face. I want to kick him out of the goddamned car right there in the rain. "Who needs you?" I tell him. "Who the hell needs a kid like you on his team?" Feel the rage going up and down my body.

CREATING COPING THOUGHTS—Worksheet

Complete the following for each significant trigger thought in an anger situation.

1. Trigger thoughts that inflame my anger:

a.

b.

c.

2. Anger distortions that underlie my trigger thoughts:

a.

b.

c.

3. Counterresponse plan for each of my trigger thoughts (e.g., looking for exceptions, alternative explanations, preferences instead of shoulds, etc.). Revised trigger thought based on each counterresponse plan.

a. Counterresponse plan:

Revised trigger thought:

b. Counterresponse plan:

Revised trigger thought:

c. Counterresponse plan:

Revised trigger thought:

4. Helpful coping thoughts (see General Coping Thoughts List earlier in this chapter):

a.

b.

c.

CREATING COPING THOUGHTS—Worksheet

Complete the following for each significant trigger thought in an anger situation.

1. Trigger thoughts that inflame my anger:

a.

b.

c.

2. Anger distortions that underlie my trigger thoughts:

a.

b.

c.

3. Counterresponse plan for each of my trigger thoughts (e.g., looking for exceptions, alternative

explanations, preferences instead of shoulds, etc.).
Revised trigger thought based on each counterresponse plan.

a. Counterresponse plan:

Revised trigger thought:

b. Counterresponse plan:

Revised trigger thought:

c. Counterresponse plan:

Revised trigger thought:

4. Helpful coping thoughts (see General Coping
Thoughts List earlier in this chapter):

a.

b.

c.

The sequence for this anger inoculation set is the
same as the one used in the last chapter with
moderate-to-high anger scenes. Begin by relaxing,
then visualize the scene and let the anger build. Once

you've achieved a level of anger, remember to *stay in the scene* and use your coping strategies. Do the entire series (four to six alternating repetitions of each scene) on two separate occasions.

Here's an example from Cheryl, a thirty-eight-year-old waitress who lives with her younger sister, Patti. She's already done the preparation by identifying trigger thoughts and distortions, and figuring out coping countermeasures.

She begins by visualizing a scene at the beach. Warm sun, slight breeze coming in from the ocean, the salty air, and sounds of seagulls complete the picture. When she finds herself feeling quite relaxed, she's ready to move on.

CLICK. It's Saturday night, close to the end of my shift at the restaurant. My feet are killing me from waiting tables all day. Every time I go into the kitchen for an order, I smell the grease on the grill going rancid. I hate this lousy job, and all the cheapskate customers with their measly tips. Beginning to get angry, I feel my stomach start to churn.

Then there's this disgusting family of four. The kids have a water fight and I have to clean up the spilled glasses. Goddamn kids running all over the place, driving me crazy. I'm gritting my teeth. Parents letting their kids run amok. They shouldn't be allowed to have kids. Then they tell me the kids are wild because the food is so late. They tell me to hurry it up. Why the hell are they eating in a restaurant in the first place with these little monsters? Whole body like a coiled spring.

Staying with the imagery of the scene, and trembling slightly with rage, Cheryl starts her coping strategies. First, some deep breathing. Then, "They were just kids having a good time." Cue-controlled relaxation. Starting to feel calmer. "I'm under control. This won't affect me." More deep breathing. Only when she feels completely relaxed does Cheryl let go of the restaurant scene. Immediately she returns to the beach, relaxing in the warm air, taking a few deep breaths.

CLICK. Sunday afternoon and I'm home alone, listening to jazz on the radio. Patti is out having a picnic with her boyfriend. I go into the kitchen and find that she left the breakfast dishes in the sink for me to clean up. My jaw tightens. "Who does she think I am? The goddamn maid?"

Looking through my closet, I discover that Patti borrowed my new sweater without even asking me. I think, "She's always taking advantage of me." Boy, that makes me mad. I don't know why I put up with that selfish bitch. I slam the closet door, picturing her face on the other side.

Holding on to the image of the scene, and still seething inside, Cheryl begins to breathe deeply. She practices relaxation without tension, focusing on her jaw. Now some coping thoughts: "I can handle this. Just breathe and relax." Cue-controlled relaxation. Cheryl decides to set some limits with Patti. "I don't have to be a victim." More deep breathing, and finally relaxed again.

Anger Inoculation—Extreme Anger Situations

This is the last, and perhaps the most important, phase of the anger inoculation process—the one that may save your life. Develop two scenes where provocation can lead to anger scores in the 85–100 SUDS range. Use the Creating Anger Scenes Worksheet to fully flesh out the details. As before, identify potential trigger thoughts and anger distortions. Next, use the Creating Coping Thoughts Worksheets to prepare your coping strategy.

CREATING ANGER SCENES—Worksheet

Extreme (85–100 SUDS) Anger Scenes

Instructions: In the spaces provided below, fill in the details of two situations in which you would

---

experience extreme levels of anger. Include details about the physical environment and what other people are saying and doing. Also describe your own trigger thoughts, feelings, and physiological reactions.

Extreme Anger Situation 1:

[Space Left Intentionally Blank in the Original Source]

Extreme Anger Situation 2:

[Space Left Intentionally Blank in the Original Source]

CREATING COPING THOUGHTS—Worksheet

Complete the following for each significant trigger thought in an anger situation.

1. Trigger thoughts that inflame my anger:

a.

b.

c.

2. Anger distortions that underlie my trigger thoughts:

a.

b.

c.

3. Counterresponse plan for each of my trigger thoughts (e.g., looking for exceptions, alternative explanations, preferences instead of shoulds, etc.). Revised trigger thought based on each counterresponse plan.

a. Counterresponse plan:

Revised trigger thought:

b. Counterresponse plan:

Revised trigger thought:

c. Counterresponse plan:

Revised trigger thought:

4. Helpful coping thoughts (see General Coping Thoughts List earlier in this chapter):

a.

b.

c.

CREATING COPING THOUGHTS—Worksheet

Complete the following for each significant trigger thought in an anger situation.

1. Trigger thoughts that inflame my anger:

a.

b.

c.

2. Anger distortions that underlie my trigger thoughts:

a.

b.

c.

3. Counterresponse plan for each of my trigger thoughts (e.g., looking for exceptions, alternative explanations, preferences instead of shoulds, etc.). Revised trigger thought based on each counterresponse plan.

a. Counterresponse plan:

Revised trigger thought:

b. Counterresponse plan:

Revised trigger thought:

c. Counterresponse plan:

Revised trigger thought:

4. Helpful coping thoughts (see General Coping Thoughts List earlier in this chapter):

a.

b.

c.

When you feel fully prepared, follow the same sequence that you used in the last set. Begin by relaxing completely. Visualize the scene, and let the anger build up as much as possible. Hold on to the scene and start to implement your coping strategies. Maintain the scene until you've managed to relax, and only then click off the first scene. Return briefly to your relaxation imagery, take a few deep breaths, and move on to the second scene.

Do the entire series (four to six alternating repetitions of each scene) on two occasions.

Homework

1. Continue to track your anger experiences and coping efforts using Anger Log III.

2. Continue to practice cue-controlled relaxation whenever stressed. By this time, it should feel as easy as a hot knife cutting through butter. Also practice the three relaxation skills and note the dates in the Relaxation Log.

3. Continue to use the Creating Coping Thoughts Worksheets for any provocative situations that are still giving you some difficulty.

4. Make sure you've completed two entire series (four to six alternating repetitions of each scene) for both high and extreme anger level scenes.

5. Implement plans on Target Problems Worksheet. (Image 11.1, 11.2)

Anger Log III

Provocative Situation Sensory Input (Objective data from what you hear, see, and touch)	The Screen (Your conclusions, assumptions, interpretations, beliefs, and trigger thoughts)	Anger Rating 0–100	Coping Strategies Breathing, relaxation, coping thoughts, coping behaviors.	Anger Rating 0–100	Outcomes Rating −10 to +10 Self	Others

Image 11.1

Relaxation Log II

Date	Relaxation Imagery	Cue-Controlled Relaxation	Relaxation without Tension

Image 11.2: INSTRUCTIONS: Put a check mark under the relaxation exercises completed on each date.

TARGET PROBLEMS—Worksheet

Instructions: In the spaces provided below, fill in the identified target problem and the steps that you'll take to deal with it differently in the future.

Target Problem:

[Space Left Intentionally Blank in the Original Source]

1. Strategy for using coping skills:

[Space Left Intentionally Blank in the Original Source]

2. Intervention point (red flag event):

[Space Left Intentionally Blank in the Original Source]

3. Foolproof coping response:

[Space Left Intentionally Blank in the Original Source]

TARGET PROBLEMS—Worksheet

Instructions: In the spaces provided below, fill in the identified target problem and the steps that you'll take to deal with it differently in the future.

Target Problem:

[Space Left Intentionally Blank in the Original Source]

1. Strategy for using coping skills:

[Space Left Intentionally Blank in the Original Source]

2. Intervention point (red flag event):

[Space Left Intentionally Blank in the Original Source]

3. Foolproof coping response:

[Space Left Intentionally Blank in the Original Source]

TARGET PROBLEMS—Worksheet

Instructions: In the spaces provided below, fill in the identified target problem and the steps that you'll take to deal with it differently in the future.

Target Problem:

[Space Left Intentionally Blank in the Original Source]

1. Strategy for using coping skills:

[Space Left Intentionally Blank in the Original Source]

2. Intervention point (red flag event):

[Space Left Intentionally Blank in the Original Source]

3. Foolproof coping response:

[Space Left Intentionally Blank in the Original Source]

CHAPTER 12

PROBLEM-SOLVING COMMUNICATION

This chapter will help you to reduce anger experiences by focusing on improving two vital skills: problem solving and communication. A useful place to begin is by examining three different coping styles: passive, aggressive, and assertive.

Coping Styles

The *passive* coping style is characterized by a desire to avoid offending people at all costs. It simply feels too scary to push for what you want if it conflicts in any way with the needs of others. Often this means saying nothing—certainly nothing about your own wants and needs. At best, you express your wants indirectly. When you need to set limits, you tend to do it by avoiding the situation or just by dragging your feet. The advantage of this coping strategy is that people will rarely be angry at you, since on the surface you appear good, sweet, and compliant. The downside, of course, is that people don't see you for who you really are. You're like the invisible man. You never get what *you* want, and often feel overwhelmed by the demands of others. What you *do* get is the opportunity to carry a load of resentment because no one seems to see or acknowledge what's important to you.

The *aggressive* coping style is characterized by pushing people around, loudly demanding that you get things your way, and punishing people who don't give you what you want. The advantage of this coping strategy is that aggressive people often *do* get what they want. This might mean having things go their way regarding chores at home, or getting the last fresh rye bread at the bakery.

There is, however, a downside as well to the aggressive coping style. The people you try to intimidate and push around will find some way to retaliate, either directly through confrontation or indirectly through avoidance. Confrontation leads to escalation and the dangers of a knockdown-drag-out fight (either physically or psychologically). Avoidance leads to a feeling of isolation and loneliness. And, the aggressive person can never be quite sure if even those close to him/her are cooperating out of love or fear.

A note about the "passive-aggressive" style: Inside every "long-suffering," passive-coping-style person is a lot of anger. When you're afraid to ask directly for what you want, resentment and pain build up inside. A "nice-guy," passive coping style leaves you feeling stuck and helpless, until the pressure builds to the breaking point. Then, any convenient trigger will serve to precipitate a vicious outburst—often indirect, yet lethal nonetheless.

The *assertive* coping style, which we recommend, is characterized by the belief that everyone has the right to express their own legitimate needs. You *are* allowed to say what you want, express feelings, stand up for your rights, and set appropriate limits. All this can be accomplished without violating the rights of others, who, by the way, also have a right to express their needs.

The assertive style allows you to work toward a settlement without anger. It makes it possible to seek a solution where both parties get something they want. The assertive style allows you to protect yourself without blaming others, and lets you set limits without turning other people off. Being assertive (rather than passive or aggressive) works well in every aspect of interpersonal interaction, whether it be struggles about money, conflicts at work, or intimate issues like sexuality. Clear, direct, and nonattacking communication will usually bring the best results.

In order to clarify these different coping styles, here are several examples of real-life situations.

Mark goes to a convenience store, picks up a six-pack of soda, and pays for it at the counter. As he's leaving the store, mentally reviewing the change he got from his ten-dollar bill, and with one foot out the door, he suddenly realizes that he's a dollar short. What does he do?

If Mark habitually used a passive coping style, he would probably say something to himself like, "Oh well, it's only a dollar. Maybe I made the mistake, and the line at the counter is awfully long." He would leave the store having avoided a potentially unpleasant confrontation. But Mark would carry a residual amount of resentment, wondering if the clerk was really trying to rip him off.

If Mark were the kind of person who used an aggressive coping style, he would respond in a different way. He'd probably whirl around, push his way back to the front of the line, and in a loud voice demand his money. "You don't even know how to make correct change. I'm a dollar short and you better give it to me." Mark would probably get his dollar, but he would also be met with hostility and resentment on future visits to the store.

But Mark is a person who uses an assertive coping style. He returns to the counter and waits until the clerk has finished with the next customer. Then, speaking up briskly, he says to the clerk, "I think that you've made a mistake. The change that you gave me is a dollar short. (Showing the change in his hand)

I gave you a ten-dollar bill." If the clerk refuses to make the correction, then Mark would say, "Please let me speak with your manager."

Another example comes from Joan, who has a friend (Sally) in need of a ride. Joan has a car, but her friend does not, and since they're both going to the same meeting, she agrees to give Sally a lift. When Joan arrives, her friend is not ready—she's just getting out of the shower. It's clear that, unless Sally really gets herself in gear, they won't get to the meeting on time.

If Joan were using a passive coping style, she would just stand around encouraging Sally to "hurry up," or try to help her find her shoes. As the time drags on, Joan would feel her stomach tighten, knowing that they would be late for the meeting, and building up resentment that would resurface later.

If Joan habitually used an aggressive coping style, she would probably say to Sally, "I'm getting god-damn sick of waiting. I'm going to the meeting and you can call a cab," slamming the door and leaving her friend in the lurch.

If Joan used an assertive coping style, she'd say, "Look, Sally, I really want to get to the meeting on time. I can wait for five minutes, but if you're not ready by then I'll have to leave. If you want, I'll call a cab for you before I go." Joan gets to the meeting on time, while giving her friend as much support and help as possible.

Assertive Statements

An assertive message is characterized by the use of the three "F's": facts, feelings, and fair requests.

"Just the *facts*, ma'am," is a familiar phrase from a popular detective drama of the sixties. Joe Friday was right. The first component of an assertive statement is an objective description of what you observe—things you see, hear, or notice. It presents the facts, as you perceive them, without making judgments, trying to place blame, or guessing at the intentions of the other person.

Here are some examples of factual observations that are not tainted by judgments or blame.

- "I notice that the sink is full of the dirty dishes from last night's dinner."

- "I see that the videos that we rented are still on the table near the door, waiting to be returned."

- "It looks like the grass on the front lawn is getting pretty high."

Sometimes it's hard to separate the facts from the feelings, but it's the first step in reducing the anger spiral. When you state the facts, it opens up the topic for discussion, and you'll be more likely to get cooperation from the other person. By contrast, beginning a discussion with an insulting comment like, "Are you too lazy to do the dishes now?" or "Lame brain, you forgot to return the videos and our lawn looks like a jungle," only serves to fuel your own anger. And comments like these are also likely to make the other person defensive and angry as well.

The second component of an assertive statement acknowledges your honest reaction, your personal *feelings.* It lets the other person become aware of how his/her behavior has affected you. It's important to state this in a way that avoids making the other person feel defensive. So you need to steer away from statements that are blaming or guilt slinging.

Here are some examples of statements that acknowledge personal feelings without judging or blaming others.

- "When I come home from work and find dirty dishes in the kitchen sink, I feel angry."

- "When you spend much of your free time either watching TV or on the Internet, I feel lonely and resentful. I miss you."

- "When we go to a party and you ignore me, paying attention to other men, I feel jealous and abandoned."

The last—and most important—part of the assertive statement is making a *fair request.* This is basically just saying what you want. There are, however, some guidelines that will make this part of the assertive statement more effective. First, make a *specific* request, and see to it that it's reasonably "doable." "I want you to be a millionaire," although specific, and an understandable desire, does not meet the criterion. "I want us to take three weeks off this summer and spend it in the mountains," is more like it.

Another important thing to remember is to make just *one* request at a time. It may be true that you want your wife to cook more French meals, spend less money on antiques, be more supportive of your career aspirations, make the azaleas bloom, and model Victoria's Secret intimate apparel. But if you bring these issues up all at once, she's bound to feel overwhelmed, criticized, and attacked.

Finally, a fair request is characterized by the fact that it seeks a *behavioral change.* It's useless to ask people to change their attitudes, values, or feelings. For example, it's reasonable for you to ask your husband to attend the office Christmas party, and he may agree to go for your sake. But asking him to *want* to go is an exercise in futility.

Now, putting it all together, here are some examples of complete assertive statements.

- "When I drove the car to work this morning I noticed that the gas tank read almost empty. (Facts) I felt annoyed and angry. (Feelings) When you use the car on the weekend, I would like you to make sure that you refill the tank, so I won't be inconvenienced." (Fair request)

- "You spend a lot of time at work, and even bring more work home with you to do on the weekends. (Facts) I feel lonely and miss our intimate times together. (Feelings) I would like to make a date with you for a quiet, romantic dinner this weekend." (Fair request)

Consequences

When you don't get results by using all the elements of assertive communication—facts, feelings, and fair request—it may be time to add a more forceful component. In the absence of willing cooperation, it might be necessary to add *consequences* to the equation.

Some people will be naturally motivated to go along with your assertive statements. They might value your friendship, or seek to maintain your continued good-will. They might see the fairness in your request, or just want to make you happy. But when people aren't motivated to meet your needs, you'll have to up the ante by providing some form of reinforcement. Using positive reinforcement (rewards) is best, simply because it usually works better than punishment, which tends to create resistance and resentment.

Unfortunately, there are times when positive rewards just won't do the job. No amount of praise or promised goodies will get the results you want. One solution is to institute consequences in the form of sanctions. Simply put, this means the other person will have to pay a price for not going along with what you want. The purpose of applying sanctions is to motivate the other person to cooperate with you or to respect your boundaries. Used judiciously, appropriate sanctions can help you get your needs met without anger.

Here are four rules for using consequences most effectively.

1.   1. **Consequences should be specific.** Be precise about exactly what behavior will trigger the consequence. And be precise about what will happen next. Vague threats like, "If you don't stop bugging me, you'll be sorry," don't give the other person enough information and are unlikely to

get results. A better formulation is, "If you don't stop calling me several times a day, I'll use my answering machine to screen calls, and won't talk to you for twenty-four hours after your last call."

2.   2. **Consequences should be reasonable.** Setting reasonable consequences helps you feel in control, and it allows other people to make sensible decisions. Avoid setting consequences that involve threats of violence or public humiliation. For example, from a mother to her teenage son: "If you don't watch your mouth I'm going to slap you silly." These types of unreasonable sanctions will tend to make people angry, and they'll be less likely to want to cooperate with you. A better reformulation of the mother-son example is, "If you speak to me again in a disrespectful manner, there'll be no allowance this week."

3.   3. **Consequences should be consistent.** If you've said that you're going to do something, like not respond to pestering phone calls, then you have to do it. And do it *every time* the situation comes up. If you don't follow through, the other person will learn not to take you seriously. Being consistent will teach the other person to respect you and your limits, both now and in the future.

4.   4. **Be sure that you can live with the results yourself.** That means, don't bite off your nose to spite your face. It doesn't make sense to try to get rid of the ant problem by dynamiting your house. The consequences you set should be problematic for the other person, not for you. Bob's divorced mother, Marion, told him that she would not fly out for his college graduation unless he shaved off what she called "that silly beard that makes you look like a bum." He decided that it was time for him to take a stand for independence. Besides, his girlfriend really thought the beard was cute. True to her word, Marion boycotted the graduation, leaving her ex-husband as the sole family representative. Dad had a great time with his son—it turned out to be a real bonding experience. To this day, Marion still regrets missing an important milestone in her son's life, and the rift it created in their relationship.

A cautionary word about making dramatic ultimatums: Be careful about using consequences like threatening to file for a divorce or kill yourself. Although these statements may seem appropriate in the heat of battle, they usually end up hurting you more, and they rarely get you what you want anyway.

Exercise: Practicing Assertiveness

On the Assertive Scripts Worksheets provided, write out an assertive script for two problematic situations in your life. Be sure to include all the elements of facts, feelings, and fair request, and a consequence that meets all the criteria mentioned above. Finally, we want you to make a commitment to change by setting a date and time for implementation.

Negotiation

Another way to minimize angry interactions is to learn how to *negotiate* when there is a conflict of interest or needs. This isn't easy, because it requires that you listen and try to understand the other person's point of view. It's much easier to simply picture the other person as wrong or stupid. Then, all you have to do is convince them, by any means possible, that you're right and they should do it your way.

Negotiation requires that you start with the premise that the other person's needs are as important to him/her as yours are to you. Trying to angrily bully your way into getting what you want will usually not get others to change their point of view. When you have a conflict of needs, negotiation allows you to find a middle ground where both of you can get some of what you want.

There are six steps to a successful negotiation:

1. **Know what it is that you want.** This isn't as easy as it sounds. Sure, you "want to be happy," but what exactly does that mean? You need to be as specific as possible.

   "I want us to go to Maine for two weeks this summer."

2. **State what you want in behavioral terms.** This means saying what, specifically, you want the other person to do or not do.

   "I want you to wash the dishes before watching any TV."

   "I don't want you to work late at the office."

3. **Listen to the other person's point of view.** The purpose of this step is to gather information so that you can understand his position, not to argue. Use active listening skills such as asking questions, clarifying, and paraphrasing what you think the other person is trying to say. Understanding a point of view doesn't mean that you have to agree with it. Having

gotten this far, you can now take the next step, which is...

4. **Make a proposal.** Your proposal should take into account what the other person needs or wants in this situation. What's in it for him or her to do what you want? This may take some creative thinking and a flexible attitude.

5. **Ask for a counterproposal.** If the other person doesn't like your proposal, encourage him or her to come up with an alternative. Remember, you're trying to come up with something that you both can live with.

6. **Achieve a compromise.** This is the heart of the negotiation process. In some situations, you might say something like, "It's really important to me that we do it this way now. What would it take for you to go along this time?" Here are some sample compromise solutions:

   • "When the kids are in my house, I'll make the rules for watching TV. When they're at your house, you make the rules."
   • "Let's try it my way for week and see if it works. If you don't like it, we'll go back to doing it the old way."
   • "When you're driving we'll do it your way, and when I'm driving we'll do it my way."

- "Let's split the difference."
- "If we do it my way this time, I'll agree to do it your way next time."

ASSERTIVE SCRIPTS—Worksheet 1

In the spaces provided below, begin by sketching out a problematic situation in your life that needs to change. Then, write out in detail an assertive script to make that happen. Be sure to fill in all the elements of facts, feelings, and fair request. Next, add a consequence that is specific, reasonable, and one that you can consistently apply without hurting yourself. Finally, write in a date and time when you plan to implement this plan.

Problematic Situation 1:

[Space Left Intentionally Blank in the Original Source]

Assertive Script

FACTS:

[Space Left Intentionally Blank in the Original Source]

FEELINGS:

[Space Left Intentionally Blank in the Original Source]

FAIR REQUEST:

[Space Left Intentionally Blank in the Original Source]

CONSEQUENCES:

[Space Left Intentionally Blank in the Original Source]

DATE & TIME OF IMPLEMENTATION:

[Space Left Intentionally Blank in the Original Source]

ASSERTIVE SCRIPTS—Worksheet 2

In the spaces provided below, begin by sketching out a problematic situation in your life that needs to change. Then, write out in detail an assertive script to make that happen. Be sure to fill in all the elements of facts, feelings, and fair request. Next, add a consequence that is specific, reasonable, and one that you can consistently apply without hurting yourself. Finally, write in a date and time when you plan to implement this plan.

Problematic Situation 2:

[Space Left Intentionally Blank in the Original Source]

Assertive Script

FACTS:

[Space Left Intentionally Blank in the Original Source]

FEELINGS:

[Space Left Intentionally Blank in the Original Source]

FAIR REQUEST:

[Space Left Intentionally Blank in the Original Source]

CONSEQUENCES:

[Space Left Intentionally Blank in the Original Source]

DATE & TIME OF IMPLEMENTATION:

[Space Left Intentionally Blank in the Original Source]

Setting Limits

Every day, you are bombarded with requests. Some of them, like going to lunch with a friend, are requests that you are glad to agree to do. Then there are all the others. Incessant calls from telemarketers trying to sell you something. Subtle requests from your boss to volunteer for a new project or put in some unpaid overtime. A call from your sister trying to guilt-trip you into taking care of your invalid father on the East Coast.

The ability to say no is a critical skill. Saying no sends a message to the world that you have your own needs, wishes, and priorities. That you are able to defend yourself against other people's demands. A statement of your own boundaries lets other people know that you're not a pushover. That you're worthy of respect, and that you value your own needs alongside the needs of others.

It is the people who can't set limits who are at risk for experiencing chronic anger. They feel taken advantage of, helpless in the face of the demands others make on their time, space, or money. They can feel like a prisoner in an intimate relationship, giving, giving, giving, all the time. They expend all their energy on people or activities that give them little pleasure or satisfaction, and they end up having little time for those things that could provide some real happiness.

There are three basic steps for setting limits:

1. **Acknowledging the other person's needs.** First, you may need to get more information about what the other person wants. Feel free to ask specific questions. What exactly is entailed in a request to "help out with the party," "be more intimate," or "advertise the new product"? Once you understand what is being requested, you can rephrase and repeat it back. This assures the other person that you have heard correctly.

2. **Stating your own position.** This is your reason for setting the limit. It may include your feelings, preferences, or perception of the circumstances. State your position without apologizing, as confidently and assertively as possible. Just describe what is true or right for you, without putting yourself down. "I need to rest this weekend." "I don't like playing golf."

3. **Saying no.** This is the essence of setting a limit. "No thanks." "I don't want to do that." "I've decided not to go." "It just doesn't feel right for me." "I'm not willing to drive."

Here are some examples of setting limits:

- "I understand that you need help with the party, and you want me to do all the shopping. (Acknowledging) I don't have the time next weekend. I'm working on a voter registration drive. (Your position) So, I won't be able to help you." (Saying no)

- "I'm aware that you feel attracted to me. (Acknowledging) I feel flattered, and enjoy spending time with you—but just as a friend. (Your position) I don't want to have a sexual relationship with you." (Saying no)

- "When you said that you wanted help to advertise the new product, you meant for me to create a full-blown ad campaign, including a color brochure. (Acknowledging) My other deadlines and commitments don't allow me the necessary time to do this project. (Your position) I have to ask you to give this project to someone else." (Saying no)

Exercise: Setting Limits

On the Setting Limits Worksheet provided, we want you to write out two limit-setting scripts, following the model provided above. Focus on *current* problem situations where you need to set a boundary, and commit yourself to implementing these ideas at the next available opportunity.

Saying no and setting limits can be difficult to accomplish at first—especially if you're not used to standing up for yourself. Here are some suggestions that will make it easier to get started:

Don't apologize. When you apologize for setting a limit, it communicates to the other person that you don't feel that you have the right to take care of yourself. Excessive apologies will invite the other person to put more pressure on you or ask for a different favor to "make it up" to them.

Don't put yourself down. Saying things like "I can't help you because ... I'm too weak ... clumsy ... afraid..." is not a good way to set a limit. The other person will try to convince you that you *can* do it, leaving you stuck with having to prove that you can't. Saying "I won't" or "I don't want to" is a much better strategy because it leaves the other person less room to argue with you.

Be aware of voice and body language. When you set a limit, look the other person in the eye. If you're on the telephone, speak with a clear, confident voice. You want your tone of voice and body posture to match your assertive statement.

Delay your response. If you're someone who tends to automatically say yes to things, stall for time. You'll probably think more clearly without the pressure of an immediate response. Tell them, "I'll let you know this afternoon," or "I'll have to get back to you on that."

Be specific. If you don't want to say no outright, be clear about exactly what you are and are not willing to do. "I'm willing to review your design for the brochure, but I won't get involved in the production end." "I'm willing to bring a bottle of wine to the party, but I can't make the salad."

SETTING LIMITS—Worksheet

In the spaces provided below, write out two scripts for saying no in a current problematic situation.

Situation 1

Acknowledge:

[Space Left Intentionally Blank in the Original Source]

State your position:

[Space Left Intentionally Blank in the Original Source]

Set limit:

[Space Left Intentionally Blank in the Original Source]

Next implementation opportunity:

[Space Left Intentionally Blank in the Original Source]

Situation 2

Acknowledge:

[Space Left Intentionally Blank in the Original Source]

State your position:

[Space Left Intentionally Blank in the Original Source]

> Set limit:
>
> [Space Left Intentionally Blank in the Original Source]
>
> Next implementation opportunity:
>
> [Space Left Intentionally Blank in the Original Source]

Dealing with Criticism

Criticism can be very painful. It can evoke memories from childhood when your behavior was minutely scrutinized for mistakes. Then you were judged and made to feel wrong, bad, guilty, and worthless. Each of these feelings has the potential for triggering anger, which is used to avoid and cover up the painful emotions.

There is a way of hearing criticism that can be beneficial to you. Accept the comment as feedback, separate out what is appropriate and useful, and disregard what is not. Here are the steps you need to take.

First, *stop the attack.* Don't allow yourself to be verbally battered by angry, abusive attacks from others. Even if you are wrong, or feel guilty about the situation, you don't deserve to be kicked around. If the other person continues to attack you, despite your request to stop, you can call for a time-out and walk away.

Whenever Sharon called her mother, Etta, she was inevitably subjected to a scathing critique of her child-rearing skills. Nothing Sharon did seemed to be right, from the way she fed her children to the clothes they wore. Etta not only gave advice freely, she also yelled at her daughter, calling her an incompetent mother. Sharon would leave each telephone call feeling devastated. Eventually, with the help of a therapist, she learned how to handle the situation. Whenever Etta started to yell or call her names, Sharon would say, "Mother, please stop shouting or I'll hang up." If her mother continued, Sharon was instructed to say, "Oh, well. Gotta go now. Bye," and hang up. She would then leave the house so that she couldn't hear the phone ring every ten minutes.

Next, remind yourself that what you're hearing is only *one person's opinion* about a specific aspect of your behavior. The criticism is about something you've done, not about who you are. The report that you submitted may be deemed "worthless" by your supervisor, but that doesn't mean that you are a worthless person, or that all your work in the past has been worthless. Accept the fact that you don't always do your best job, often because of being rushed or not having all the information you need.

Some criticism can be constructive and helpful. Before you fly into a rage or slink away in embarrassment, make sure you know exactly what the critic is trying to tell you. In order to get the most value out of the situation, you will have to *ask for more information.* Although it's uncomfortable to encourage the critic, probing for more information may provide you with the useful feedback you need to improve future performance—or your relationship.

When Jim wrote the report for his company, he included lots of historical analysis and comparisons to other industries. His supervisor, Bob, returned the report to him, saying it was "useless." Jim felt hurt and devastated, but he was also curious. He asked Bob what exactly he would have liked to see in the report. It turns out that what was wanted was a current market analysis, comparison with other companies in the same industry, and projections for the next five years. The report Jim submitted, although good background material, was indeed useless. What Jim learned is that Bob doesn't always communicate his needs well. Next time he will ask more questions and get all the information he needs before writing a report.

Trevor thought that his relationship with MaryLou was going pretty well, despite fights now and then. So he was really surprised and hurt when MaryLou became critical and attacked him, apparently out of the blue. "You're just never there for me. All you care about is yourself and your own needs." Gathering courage, Trevor asked her what she meant. "Remember last year, when you broke your ankle and it was in a cast for six weeks? I was at your house every other day, cleaning up, cooking your food, and waiting on you hand and foot. I've been sick with the flu for more than a week and you just go on with your life, and don't even come by to see how I am." Trevor was indeed "clueless," but now he has some more information. MaryLou would feel cared for if he paid more attention to her and did some things to help her out when she was down.

There are three techniques that you can use to deflect criticism, prevent escalation, and disarm the critic.

1. **Clouding** is a strategy in which you partially agree with the criticism without accepting it completely. This requires that you listen carefully to the critic and agree with the part of the criticism that you feel is accurate. Other options are to agree in principle, or agree in probability.

For example, the *criticism* might be, "You spend money like it grows on trees. At this rate we'll be penniless in no time." You can *agree in part* by saying, "Yeah, we have been spending more money since we bought those horses." Or you could *agree in principle,* by saying, "I think you're right, it's not a good idea to spend too much money." Lastly, you could choose to *agree in probability* by saying something like, "It's probably true that we're spending quite a bit right now."

2. Making an **assertive preference** is a way of shutting off the critic completely. You use this technique by acknowledging the criticism, but dis-agreeing with it. There's no need to give a lengthy explanation or rationale for your behavior—you simply state that that's the way you want to do things. This technique assumes an equal power situation and is a very effective way of stopping further discussion without attacking the other person. And you can do it without getting angry.

For example, if the criticism is, "That's a dumb way to deal with your kids coming home after curfew," you can respond with an assertive preference statement by saying, "I hear that you don't agree with how I'm handling this situation, but I prefer to do it this way." If the critic tries to continue by pointing out the dangers of doing it your way, you can respond by saying, "Thanks for your concern, but I'm willing to take that risk."

3. You can make a **content-to-process shift** to prevent a discussion from heating up into a full-blown conflagration, or when you think that underlying feelings are fueling the fire. When you make a content-to-process shift, the focus of the discussion changes from the issue (content) to what's going on inside you or the quality of the interaction (process). It allows you to get to the real or more important issue that lies at the bottom of the conflict.

For example, "I know that you like me to look good in public, but we're always arguing about how much money I spend on clothes. I end up feeling accused and attacked by you. What's going on between us that we're feeling angry all the time?"

Exercise: Dealing with Criticism

Use the worksheet on the next page to prepare some more effective ways to deal with criticism. Begin by writing a description of a recent provocative scene in which you felt criticized and attacked. Then, write out what words or actions you would have employed to stop the attack. Next, write what specific questions you would have asked to learn more about the other person's needs, feelings, or problems. Finally, write down some ways in which you could have used clouding, assertive preference, or content-to-process shift to deflect the attack.

Homework

1. Monitor anger and coping responses on Anger Log III.

2. Use the Creating Coping Thoughts Worksheet to develop better anger management responses following situations where you lapsed into anger.

DEALING WITH CRITICISM—Worksheet

In the space below, write a description of a recent provocative scene in which you felt criticized and attacked. Then, *in retrospect,* fill out the rest of the worksheet with strategies that you could have used to change the outcome.

Provocative scene involving criticism:

[Space Left Intentionally Blank in the Original Source]

If you decided to stop the attack, how could you accomplish it? Words:

[Space Left Intentionally Blank in the Original Source]

Actions:

[Space Left Intentionally Blank in the Original Source]

If you wanted to learn more about the other person's position, what specific questions would you ask to ascertain the following:

Feelings:

[Space Left Intentionally Blank in the Original Source]

Problems:

[Space Left Intentionally Blank in the Original Source]

What they want:

[Space Left Intentionally Blank in the Original Source]

If you wanted to deflect the attack, how would you use: Clouding:

248

Anger Log III

| Provocative Situation | | Anger Rating 0–100 | Coping Strategies | Anger Rating 0–100 | Outcomes Rating -10 to +10 | |
Sensory Input (Objective data from what you hear, see, and touch)	The Screen (Your conclusions, assumptions, interpretations, beliefs, and trigger thoughts)		Breathing, relaxation, coping thoughts, coping behaviors.		Self	Others

Image 12.1

[Space Left Intentionally Blank in the Original Source]

Assertive preference:

[Space Left Intentionally Blank in the Original Source]

Content-to-process shift:

[Space Left Intentionally Blank in the Original Source] (Image 12.1)

CREATING COPING THOUGHTS—Worksheet

Complete the following for each significant trigger thought in an anger situation.

1. Trigger thoughts that inflame my anger:

a.

b.

c.

2. Anger distortions that underlie my trigger thoughts:

a.

b.

c.

3. Counterresponse plan for each of my trigger thoughts (e.g., looking for exceptions, alternative explanations, preferences instead of shoulds, etc.). Revised trigger thought based on each counterresponse plan.

a. Counterresponse plan:

Revised trigger thought:

b. Counterresponse plan:

Revised trigger thought:

c. Counterresponse plan:

Revised trigger thought:

4. Helpful coping thoughts (see General Coping Thoughts List earlier in this chapter):

a.

b.

c.

CREATING COPING THOUGHTS—Worksheet

Complete the following for each significant trigger thought in an anger situation.

1. Trigger thoughts that inflame my anger:

a.

b.

c.

2. Anger distortions that underlie my trigger thoughts:

a.

b.

c.

3. Counterresponse plan for each of my trigger thoughts (e.g., looking for exceptions, alternative explanations, preferences instead of shoulds, etc.).

Revised trigger thought based on each counterresponse plan.

a. Counterresponse plan:

Revised trigger thought:

b. Counterresponse plan:

Revised trigger thought:

c. Counterresponse plan:

Revised trigger thought:

4. Helpful coping thoughts (see General Coping Thoughts List earlier in this chapter):

a.

b.

c.

CHAPTER 13

YOUR PLAN FOR REAL-LIFE COPING

This chapter will be an opportunity to synthesize much of what you've learned so far about anger management. The first step will be an exercise to help you recognize and remember the coping thoughts that have worked best for you.

Best Coping Thoughts

Look back over the three chapters where you used anger inoculation to cope with anger in visualized scenes. Review each Creating Coping Thoughts Worksheet that you filled out and write down on a separate piece of paper the coping thoughts that seemed most effective. Now go back and review the "coping efforts" column from each Anger Log III that you've completed. Add any good coping thoughts that you find in your logs to the list you're compiling.

Now it's time to turn the list you just made into something that can really help you. The Best Coping Thoughts Exercise you're about to complete will organize the random coping thoughts from your list into nine specific coping categories. The categories for best coping thoughts are:

1. **Cool thoughts.** These are simple reminders to use your relaxation skills.

2. **Problem-solving thoughts.** This type of coping thought identifies alternative solutions to a problem. Anger is just a signal to start looking for new answers.

3. **Escape routes.** These thoughts remind you to walk away from something upsetting, to remove yourself from the situation before things escalate.

4. **Self-confidence thoughts.** These remind you that you have the ability to manage your anger in provocative situations. No matter what happens, you recognize that you have the skills to cope.

5. **New explanations.** These thoughts help you identify alternative ways of thinking about people's problematic behavior. Why else might they be acting as they do? Instead of assuming that you're a target, these coping thoughts look for more benign interpretations.

6. **See the whole picture.** This type of coping thought looks for exceptions to overgeneraliza-

tions. You try to remember balancing facts or events that help you see the other person in a less negative light.

7. **Getting accurate.** These are self-reminders that encourage you to stay with the facts of a situation while avoiding any kind of magnifying or exaggerating. Getting accurate can also mean recognizing how a situation is *realistically negative,* but not awful or unbearable.

8. **Preferences, not shoulds.** This category of coping thoughts changes absolute "should" statements into simple preferences. Instead of focusing on unbendable rules for living, you soften angry expectations into personal wants and desires.

9. **People doing their best.** These coping thoughts remind you that people are trying to survive their own pain and struggles. They're trying to manage their life circumstances as best they can.

Exercise: Best Coping Thoughts*

[* Adapted from *Overcoming Situational and General Anger* by Jerry Deffenbacher and Matthew McKay.]

This exercise includes the nine categories of coping thoughts just discussed. Under each category, you'll find some examples. Then there's a space for you to fill in coping thoughts of your own (from the list you just compiled) that seem to fit that category.

When you've worked your way through all nine coping thought categories, go back and do another pass. Read each of the example coping thoughts that are included in the exercise. Put a star by any of the example coping thoughts that you think might be helpful for you.

As a final step, focus on the coping thoughts categories where you've written nothing down. Take some time to think about each of these categories and see if you can create some coping thought of your own for them. If you have difficulty, go back and look at the General Coping Thoughts list in chapter 8.

Cool Thoughts

"Just stay cool, getting all pissed off won't help."

"It's just not worth it. Take a few deep breaths and chill out."

"This too shall pass. Others have to deal with this kind of stuff without going crazy mad."

Your coping thoughts:

[Space Left Intentionally Blank in the Original Source]

Problem-Solving Thoughts

"It's not the end of the world, just a problem to be solved."

"It's okay to feel annoyed, but it's just a hassle to be dealt with."

"Develop a plan. So, the first thing I would want to do is..."

"Break the frustration down. I can deal better with it that way."

Your coping thoughts:

[Space Left Intentionally Blank in the Original Source]

Escape Routes

"I can always walk away rather than lose it totally."

"It's okay to take time out. Move away, get your act together, then come back and deal with it."

"Better to walk away than to be a screaming idiot."

"Bottom line, I walk before I hit or do something dumb."

Your coping thoughts:

[Space Left Intentionally Blank in the Original Source]

Self-Confidence Thoughts
"I can handle this—I've done it before."

"I'm hanging in and coping."

"I have what it takes to get through this hassle."

"I'm getting better at this anger management stuff."

Your coping thoughts:

[Space Left Intentionally Blank in the Original Source]

New Explanations
"They're probably just (scared, overwhelmed, not understanding, confused, out of the loop, hurting, etc.)"

"Cut them some slack. I'd hope they'd do the same for me if I were having a bad time."

Your coping thoughts:

[Space Left Intentionally Blank in the Original Source]

See the Whole Picture
"Look at the other side."

"There are exceptions. For example..."

"Time to look for some of the good for a change."

Your coping thoughts:

[Space Left Intentionally Blank in the Original Source]

Getting Accurate
"Cut the angry crap. Tell it like it is." "Just the facts."

"Tell it simple and straight."

"I'm frustrated and disappointed. Better stay there and quit while I'm only somewhat behind."

Your coping thoughts:

[Space Left Intentionally Blank in the Original Source]

Preferences, Not Shoulds

"It doesn't have to be my way, I just prefer it."

"What I want and what has to be are two different things."

"This is what I *need,* not a *should.*"

"Nobody appointed me God. So give it up. Be human and focus on your wants."

Your coping thoughts:

[Space Left Intentionally Blank in the Original Source]

People Doing Their Best

"They're doing what they know how to do."

"They're coping the best they can, all things considered."

"I don't like how they do it, but they're just trying to survive."

Your coping thoughts:

[Space Left Intentionally Blank in the Original Source]

Best Coping Behaviors

Now it's time to look back again at the "coping efforts" column of Anger Log III. This time, pay attention to how you behave in response to anger provocations. What are you doing or not doing that is different from your old anger response? Do you try to speak in a quieter voice? Do you choose words that are less inflammatory? Do you withdraw at times from a provocative situation rather than explode? Do you find a way to express your needs assertively rather than use blaming attacks? Have you on occasion suggested a solution or a compromise instead of going on the warpath?

While you may find some examples of good coping behaviors in the Anger Log, many of your best coping efforts may be in situations where you never got angry enough to write anything down. Your very success made your coping efforts easy to forget. The exercise that follows is an opportunity to record your best and most successful coping behaviors. In the space provided in the exercise, write examples from your own recent experience of each category of coping behavior. Don't be surprised if you have no examples that fit some of the categories. No one person is going to use all of these coping strategies.

Exercise: Best Coping Behaviors

1. Expressed needs in nonattacking ways. Examples:

    [Space Left Intentionally Blank in the Original Source]

2. Softened inflammatory language. Examples:

    [Space Left Intentionally Blank in the Original Source]

3. Lowered my voice. Examples:

    [Space Left Intentionally Blank in the Original Source]

4. Suggested an alternative solution or compromise. Examples:

    [Space Left Intentionally Blank in the Original Source]

5. Tried to express understanding of the other person's views. Examples:

    [Space Left Intentionally Blank in the Original Source]

6. Withdrew from a situation rather than let it escalate. Took time to think things through. Examples:

   [Space Left Intentionally Blank in the Original Source]

7. Agreed to disagree and let it go. Examples:

   [Space Left Intentionally Blank in the Original Source]

8. Described a problem without blaming the other person. Examples:

   [Space Left Intentionally Blank in the Original Source]

9. Tried to listen to the other person to get a better awareness of what they want. Examples:

   [Space Left Intentionally Blank in the Original Source]

10. Tried to change the subject so things wouldn't escalate. Examples:

    [Space Left Intentionally Blank in the Original Source]

11. Other coping behaviors:

   [Space Left Intentionally Blank in the Original Source]

Once filled in, this exercise provides you a good list of coping behaviors that work for you. You can use it as a resource and return to it again and again for ideas about how to manage your anger in difficult situations.

Advance Planning: The Key to Real-Life Anger Management

Learning to cope with visualized anger scenes is one thing. Managing your anger in the face of real-life provocations is quite another. All the practicing you've done with anger inoculation has served to give you more effective coping skills. Now it's time to make a strong commitment to use these skills where it counts—with your friends, family, and coworkers.

*Exercise: Anger Planning***

[** Adapted from *Overcoming Situational and General Anger* by Jerry Deffenbacher and Matthew McKay.]

This anger planning exercise has six sections: anger precipitants, trigger thoughts, coping thoughts, relaxation, coping behavior, and problem solving. Right now, fill in the Anger Planning Exercise using a recent provocation as an example situation. Start off by writing down all the anger precipitants in the situation. Mostly these would be the actual events, although precipitants might include memories or even feelings that preceded your anger. For trigger thoughts, write down every inflammatory thought that fueled your anger. For the coping thoughts section, we suggest that you review the Best Coping Thoughts Exercise that you completed earlier in the chapter. Try to find several that would be useful to manage your anger in this particular situation. In the relaxation section, write in the specific relaxation skill that you feel would be most effective while facing this particular provocation. Under coping behavior, try to develop at least one strategy that might keep this situation from escalating in the future. Use the list you created in the Best Coping Behaviors Exercise for ideas. Finally, in the problem-solving section, note any alternative solution or problem solving scenario you can think of. Do you have any idea of how you could structure things to avoid this problem in the future? Is there something you could say or do when you aren't upset that would alter the provocative situation in some way?

Anger Precipitants:

What events, memories, associations, or feelings preceded my anger?

[Space Left Intentionally Blank in the Original Source]

Trigger Thoughts:

What inflammatory thoughts set off my anger?

[Space Left Intentionally Blank in the Original Source]

Coping Thoughts:

Look at Best Coping Thoughts Worksheet for help.

[Space Left Intentionally Blank in the Original Source]

Relaxation:

How can I use my relaxation skills in this situation (e.g., take a deep breath before I say anything, etc.)?

[Space Left Intentionally Blank in the Original Source]

Coping Behavior:

What can I say or do that will calm things down?

[Space Left Intentionally Blank in the Original Source]

Problem Solving:

Is there a way to solve this problem and avoid conflict?

[Space Left Intentionally Blank in the Original Source]

Here's an example of how Roger, a short-order cook, completed the Anger Planning Exercise.

Anger Precipitants:

Thelma (waitress) takes a long time picking up her orders. The server shelf fills up and I have nowhere to put new orders.

Trigger Thoughts:

Where's Mrs. Molasses? She's slower than a damn double amputee. She's lazy. She's screwing me up.

Coping Thoughts:

> *Cool down, you can handle this. You can solve the problem and chill. She's probably doing the best she can.*

Relaxation:

> *Deep breath; use phrase, Let it be. Relax my tight shoulders.*

Coping Behavior:

> *Stop constantly ringing the bell and trying to get her attention; put the order under the warmer and wait till she asks for it.*

Problem Solving:

> *Ask restaurant owner about a second server shelf.*

At the end of this chapter, you'll find multiple copies of this exercise, labeled Anger Planning Worksheet. You are encouraged to fill out the worksheet for chronic provocations and anger situations you can anticipate during the coming week. Anger planning is an excellent tool to make sure you have effective responses to any upset or provocation that you can anticipate.

Homework

Anger Log III

| Provocative Situation | | Anger Rating 0–100 | Coping Strategies | Anger Rating 0–100 | Outcomes Rating -10 to +10 | |
Sensory Input (Objective data from what you hear, see, and touch)	The Screen (Your conclusions, assumptions, interpretations, beliefs, and trigger thoughts)		Breathing, relaxation, coping thoughts, coping behaviors.		Self	Others

Image 13.1

1. Continue to track your anger experiences and coping efforts using Anger Log III.

2. For any anger situation where you didn't respond adequately, fill out an Anger Planning Worksheet. Draw on your Best Coping Thoughts and Best Coping Behaviors Exercises to complete the worksheet. If you have difficulty developing appropriate coping thoughts for a specific provocation, use a Creating Coping Thoughts Worksheet. (Image 13.1)

CREATING COPING THOUGHTS—Worksheet

Complete the following for each significant trigger thought in an anger situation.

1. Trigger thoughts that inflame my anger:

a.

b.

c.

2. Anger distortions that underlie my trigger thoughts:

a.

b.

---

c.

3. Counterresponse plan for each of my trigger thoughts (e.g., looking for exceptions, alternative explanations, preferences instead of shoulds, etc.). Revised trigger thought based on each counterresponse plan.

a. Counterresponse plan:

Revised trigger thought:

b. Counterresponse plan:

Revised trigger thought:

c. Counterresponse plan:

Revised trigger thought:

4. Helpful coping thoughts (see General Coping Thoughts List earlier in this chapter):

a.

b.

c.

CREATING COPING THOUGHTS—Worksheet

Complete the following for each significant trigger thought in an anger situation.

1. Trigger thoughts that inflame my anger:

a.

b.

c.

2. Anger distortions that underlie my trigger thoughts:

a.

b.

c.

3. Counterresponse plan for each of my trigger thoughts (e.g., looking for exceptions, alternative explanations, preferences instead of shoulds, etc.). Revised trigger thought based on each counterresponse plan.

a. Counterresponse plan:

Revised trigger thought:

b. Counterresponse plan:

Revised trigger thought:

c. Counterresponse plan:

Revised trigger thought:

4. Helpful coping thoughts (see General Coping Thoughts List earlier in this chapter):

a.

b.

c.

ANGER PLANNING—Worksheet

Anger Precipitants:

What events, memories, associations, or feelings preceded my anger?

[Space Left Intentionally Blank in the Original Source]

Trigger Thoughts:

What inflammatory thoughts set off my anger?

[Space Left Intentionally Blank in the Original Source]

Coping Thoughts:

Look at Best Coping Thoughts Worksheet for help.

[Space Left Intentionally Blank in the Original Source]

Relaxation:

How can I use my relaxation skills in this situation (e.g., take a deep breath before I say anything, etc.)?

[Space Left Intentionally Blank in the Original Source]

Coping Behavior:

What can I say or do that will calm things down?

[Space Left Intentionally Blank in the Original Source]

Problem Solving:

Is there a way to solve this problem and avoid conflict?

[Space Left Intentionally Blank in the Original Source]

ANGER PLANNING—Worksheet

Anger Precipitants:

What events, memories, associations, or feelings preceded my anger?

[Space Left Intentionally Blank in the Original Source]

Trigger Thoughts:

What inflammatory thoughts set off my anger?

[Space Left Intentionally Blank in the Original Source]

Coping Thoughts:

Look at Best Coping Thoughts Worksheet for help.

[Space Left Intentionally Blank in the Original Source]

Relaxation:

How can I use my relaxation skills in this situation (e.g., take a deep breath before I say anything, etc.)?

[Space Left Intentionally Blank in the Original Source]

Coping Behavior:

What can I say or do that will calm things down?

[Space Left Intentionally Blank in the Original Source]

Problem Solving:

Is there a way to solve this problem and avoid conflict?

[Space Left Intentionally Blank in the Original Source]

CHAPTER 14

BLOCKS TO REAL-LIFE COPING

Anyone who's been on this earth more than ten minutes knows that things aren't perfect. This is never more true than when you're trying to change a habit. There are plenty of times when you'll forget or get caught up in some of the powerful reinforcers that created the habit to begin with. Your new anger management program is bound to have some spectacular failures scattered among the times you successfully cope.

Number one, don't condemn yourself. Old ways die hard. Number two, learn from your mistakes. Fill out an Anger Planning Worksheet after any occasion where your coping efforts didn't work. But perhaps most important, take a realistic look at the factors that may be blocking use of your new anger management skills. This chapter will help you do that. The exercise that follows will allow you to examine the six most common obstacles to effective anger control.

Exercise: Blocks to Real Life Coping

1. You expect to be embarrassed if people notice you practicing your relaxation skills.

You're not alone if you worry about this. But how obvious is it when you take a deep breath? To find out, try this experiment: Stand in front of a mirror and take several slow breaths using cue-controlled relaxation. Be objective. Does it look like anything more than a sigh or the deep breath that people often take in the middle of a tense situation? Most people, watching themselves take a breath in the mirror, report that it doesn't look odd. Right now, commit yourself to taking one or two deep breaths and using your cue word every time you're in an angry encounter. It will look as normal as a sigh.

2. When angry you can't remember to use your coping skills.

Most people struggle with this because anger tends to erase everything else from your mind. It's a storm that seems to blow away your best intentions and plans. Nonetheless, the problem can be overcome. What you need is a reminder to use your coping skills. When someone gets in your face, or does something that seems totally irresponsible, you can cue yourself to relax and use your coping thoughts. A simple strategy is to wear something that's unusual and acts as a reminder that you have to stop and cope. A new ring or piece of jewelry could work, or an unusual color of nail polish. Something as simple as putting your watch on the other wrist might act as a cue to use your new skills. When you do any of these things deliberately, as part of a plan to jog your memory, you improve your chances of noticing them when a situation gets hot. Additional strategies might involve using signs—on your vanity or shaving mirror. You could tape up a file card that says, "Breathe when you're pissed." Or you could put a reminder in your wallet, in your desk drawer, or by a light switch.

Right now, take a moment to look over your Anger Logs for the past few weeks. Focus on the Coping Strategies column. First off, give yourself some credit for the times you successfully coped. Every time you've replaced your old anger pattern with a new coping strategy, it represents a lot of hard work.

Second, each occasion when you've successfully coped could be a gold mine of information that would help right now. Think back. How did you *remember* to use your new coping skills? Was it spontaneous? Did someone remind you? Did you use a cue or a sign? Did you try to fix in your mind beforehand a criterion behavior—some response on your or the other person's part—that would be a signal to cope? Typical criterion behaviors could be raising your voice, a belittling or attacking tone, pointing gestures, foul language or name calling, and so on. Some criterion behaviors might even be internal events, like muscle tension or a particular negative thought.

Looking back, did you use any other strategies to remember your skills? For example, did you ever promise someone whose opinion matters that you'd try to cope more effectively in a particular target situation? Or did you ever try reminding yourself throughout the day of your commitment to cope with anger? One man actually programmed a watch to beep every hour as a way to keep his coping plans in mind.

The following chart may help you get clearer about some of the strategies you already use to remember your skills. In the left hand column of the Remembering to Cope Worksheet, write down each of your anger coping efforts from the past two weeks. Don't write a lot, just a sentence or even a couple of words to identify the incident. Then, in the right hand column, write the word or phrase that describes how you remembered to cope. Examples of memory strategies are written across the top of the worksheet, but it's okay to develop your own labels for ways *you* remember to cope.

Examine your memory strategies listed on the worksheet. Do you find that you rely on only one or two strategies? If so, you might consider testing additional strategies that seem potentially helpful. Select three anger situations that you run into with some consistency, and where you often forget to use your coping skills. Write them in the left-hand column: (Table 14.1)

Anger Provocation	Memory Strategy
1.	1.
2.	2.
3.	3.

Table 14.1

Now that you have the provocations listed, look back at the example memory strategies at the top of the Remembering to Cope Worksheet. Select one that you haven't tried before for each of the above provocations and write it in the space under Memory Strategy. Right now make a commitment to yourself to implement the selected memory strategy for each of the provocations.

3. You can't recall any coping thoughts during a provocation.

No one thinks clearly when they're upset. As you learned in the last chapter, any provocation that shows up with regularity will have a better outcome when you do some advanced planning. You can deal with such provocations using the Anger Planning Worksheet.

REMEMBERING TO COPE—Worksheet*
[* From *Overcoming Situational and General Anger* by Jerry Deffenbacher and Matthew McKay.]

Spontaneously remembered; reminded by someone; memory cue; signs; criterion behavior; promise to someone; self-reminding throughout day (Table 14.2)

Coping Efforts	Memory Strategies
1	1
2	2
3	3
4	4
5	5
6	6
7	7
8	8
9	9
10	10
11	11
12	12

Table 14.2

There are, of course, provocations you can't plan for. They come at you from out of the blue. For these you need a generic coping thought that feels strong and "right." Refer to the General Coping Thoughts list in chapter 8 to find something that might be effective as an all-purpose coping response. Write it in the space below.

Generic Coping Thought:

[Space Left Intentionally Blank in the Original Source]

Now strongly commit yourself to using this coping thought whenever you start getting upset. Memorize it. Practice recalling it throughout the day.

4. You won't be listened to if you cope successfully and stop being angry.

Many people are afraid to lose their anger. They expect no one will listen if they aren't aggressive and attacking. They're so used to getting loud that talking in a normal voice feels like they've been silenced. Paradoxically, the exact opposite is true. When you're always loud and angry, people *stop* listening. They get defensive and resistant, and they look for reasons to ignore you.

Right now, do a quick mental inventory of some of your recent anger experiences. Did you feel heard? Did the target of your anger express concern about your needs and feelings? Was your viewpoint appreciated? Chances are, if you look at it objectively, most of these anger experiences didn't have a positive outcome. People were too busy protecting themselves from your ire to really hear what you had to say.

5. When you're upset, you want to punish people for their mistakes.

If you control your anger, no one pays for their transgressions. This feeling is not uncommon. It's hard to cope with and modulate your anger when at the same time you want to use it as a weapon. But this desire, understandable as it is, has had a negative impact on your relationships and your life. That's why you've been working so hard on this program. The exercise you did in chapter 2 helped you identify the effects of your anger on both your personal and work life. Right now, in the space below, write down one reason you are ready to let go of anger as a tool for punishing wrongdoers.

[Space Left Intentionally Blank in the Original Source]

If you can't think of a single reason that feels true and motivating, this could be a serious impediment to your anger control efforts. You are strongly encouraged, in this case, to seek the help of a psychotherapist or pastoral counselor who can open this issue to deeper exploration.

6. Anger feels like the only way you can protect yourself.

Anger functions to protect you from two kinds of threats. First, anger can help you repel pressures, demands, and attacks from others. It can mobilize you to fight back. Anger also can help to block internal threats—emotions such as shame, hurt, fear, and guilt that feel as though they might overwhelm you.

When someone is really pushing you around or threatening you, anger can be an appropriate, healthy response. It's a signal for others to back off. Most of the time, however, anger is overkill. You don't need it. A clear, assertive statement is usually enough to get people to listen. Right now, make a list of the last six anger situations noted in your logs. Write a phrase to remind you of each in the left-hand column below. (Table 14.3)

Anger Situations	Assertive Alternative	Outcome + or -
1.	1.	1.
2.	2.	2.
3.	3.	3.
4.	4.	4.
5.	5.	5.

6.   6.   6

Table 14.3

Anger Log III

Provocative Situation Sensory Input (Objective data from what you hear, see, and touch)	The Screen (Your conclusions, assumptions, interpretations, beliefs, and trigger thoughts)	Anger Rating 0–100	Coping Strategies Breathing, relaxation, coping thoughts, coping behaviors.	Anger Rating 0–100	Outcomes Rating -10 to +10 Self Others	

Image 14.1

When you've finished filling in the six anger situations, go back over each one and write down in the column labeled Assertive Alternative an assertive statement you could have used to replace your angry ones. In the column marked Outcome, write + or -, depending on whether the assertive statement would likely have had a better or worse result than your anger response.

The purpose of this exercise is to get a sense of how often anger is necessary and healthy as a response to threats. People tend to find, when looking at outcomes, that few if any of the anger situations actually require anger. Most would have better results using assertive statements.

As previously noted, anger can protect you internally as well as externally. It can be an effective defense against painful emotions. In the space below, write down the feeling or feelings from which anger has historically protected you. Be honest. When you get really steamed, is there another emotion that often comes first, that seems sometimes to actually trigger your anger?

[Space Left Intentionally Blank in the Original Source]

If you often employ anger as a defense against the feeling or feelings listed above, if your reflex is to blow up rather than experience painful emotions, this is more than understandable. But it's also dangerous. While the anger is protecting you from overwhelming feelings, it is simultaneously damaging. You may need help from a trained therapist to cope more effectively with the feelings your anger has traditionally blocked.

Homework

1. Continue recording any significant anger incidents in Anger Log III, along with your coping efforts.

2. Fill out Anger Planning Worksheets (provided at the end of the chapter) for each anger situation where your coping efforts are not successful. (Image 14.1)

CREATING COPING THOUGHTS—Worksheet

Complete the following for each significant trigger thought in an anger situation.

1. Trigger thoughts that inflame my anger:

a.

b.

---

c.

2. Anger distortions that underlie my trigger thoughts:

a.

b.

c.

3. Counterresponse plan for each of my trigger thoughts (e.g., looking for exceptions, alternative explanations, preferences instead of shoulds, etc.). Revised trigger thought based on each counterresponse plan.

a. Counterresponse plan:

Revised trigger thought:

b. Counterresponse plan:

Revised trigger thought:

c. Counterresponse plan:

Revised trigger thought:

4. Helpful coping thoughts (see General Coping Thoughts List earlier in this chapter):

a.

b.

c.

CREATING COPING THOUGHTS—Worksheet

Complete the following for each significant trigger thought in an anger situation.

1. Trigger thoughts that inflame my anger:

a.

b.

c.

2. Anger distortions that underlie my trigger thoughts:

a.

b.

c.

3. Counterresponse plan for each of my trigger thoughts (e.g., looking for exceptions, alternative explanations, preferences instead of shoulds, etc.). Revised trigger thought based on each counterresponse plan.

a. Counterresponse plan:

Revised trigger thought:

b. Counterresponse plan:

Revised trigger thought:

c. Counterresponse plan:

Revised trigger thought:

4. Helpful coping thoughts (see General Coping Thoughts List earlier in this chapter):

a.

b.

c.

ANGER PLANNING—Worksheet

Anger Precipitants:

What events, memories, associations, or feelings preceded my anger?

[Space Left Intentionally Blank in the Original Source]

Trigger Thoughts:

What inflammatory thoughts set off my anger?

[Space Left Intentionally Blank in the Original Source]

Coping Thoughts:

Look at Best Coping Thoughts Worksheet for help.

[Space Left Intentionally Blank in the Original Source]

Relaxation:

How can I use my relaxation skills in this situation (e.g., take a deep breath before I say anything, etc.)?

[Space Left Intentionally Blank in the Original Source]

Coping Behavior:

What can I say or do that will calm things down?

[Space Left Intentionally Blank in the Original Source]

Problem Solving:

Is there a way to solve this problem and avoid conflict?

[Space Left Intentionally Blank in the Original Source]

ANGER PLANNING—Worksheet

Anger Precipitants:

What events, memories, associations, or feelings preceded my anger?

[Space Left Intentionally Blank in the Original Source]

Trigger Thoughts:

What inflammatory thoughts set off my anger?

[Space Left Intentionally Blank in the Original Source]

Coping Thoughts:

Look at Best Coping Thoughts Worksheet for help.

[Space Left Intentionally Blank in the Original Source]

Relaxation:

How can I use my relaxation skills in this situation (e.g., take a deep breath before I say anything, etc.)?

[Space Left Intentionally Blank in the Original Source]

Coping Behavior:

What can I say or do that will calm things down?

[Space Left Intentionally Blank in the Original Source]

Problem Solving:

Is there a way to solve this problem and avoid conflict?

[Space Left Intentionally Blank in the Original Source]

CHAPTER 15

BEING GOOD TO YOURSELF

We've discussed at other times in this book how anger is most often a response to pain. Something feels very wrong, and anger seems like a way of coping with it. Whether the distress is emotional or physical, for a moment the anger masks it.

This chapter is about dealing with distress in proactive ways so anger will be less and less needed in your life. It's about nourishing and being good to yourself. It's about creating a life where your physical and emotional well-being are high priorities.

The first step in taking better care of yourself is learning to be more aware of what we call TLC issues:

Tired/stressed

Lonely

Craving (food, peace, stimulation, meaning, etc.)

Our experience shows that at least half of all anger episodes are in some way associated with TLC problems. It's far more effective to work on TLC issues directly, as a problem to solve, than to cover the distress with angry words. You'll end up feeling a lot better, and so will those around you.

The Big Question

A simple but important discipline in anger control is to ask, every time you're starting to get hot, "What's my TLC level?"

- Am I tired or physically distressed in any way? Do I need to sit, take a break, sleep, relax my muscles?

- Am I feeling a need for contact? Would it help if I talked to someone right now? Or just spent time doing something fun with someone?

- Am I hungry for something? Do I need food or quiet or something interesting to do?

Once you identify a TLC problem, shift the focus to what you can do about it. The royal road to anger is feeling stuck and helpless, so solving TLC distress is a high priority. Don't put it off if you can help it. Make a plan right away for how and when you'll get rest, contact a friend, or do something fun. If at all possible, plan to address a TLC issue on the same day you notice it. That way relief is in sight. You can look forward to feeling better rather than feeling helpless and angry.

Put a Cork in the Self-Hating Voice

People who struggle with anger often have strong judgments about others. But that gun points both ways. They frequently reserve the most negative, hateful judgments for themselves. This self-attacking voice has been called the "pathological critic." It's usually a whole load of judgments you've internalized from things your parents said over and over. The critic calls you stupid, lazy, or selfish; it says you're ugly, crazy, incompetent, or boring.

Sometimes the pathological critic attacks you for a lot more than your parents actually said. It condemns you for what their actions *suggest* they felt toward you. For example, if they paid you little attention and rarely helped when you needed it, the critic might call you "worthless" or a "burden to everyone."

The main function of the critic is to keep you feeling as rotten as you did as a child, to keep that old negative identity intact. The critic's main weapon is a stream of vicious, negative labels. And the result of all the critic's work is a hidden world of shame and self-contempt. In the end, you're in so much pain that the slightest hurt or criticism from others feels intolerable, and you fly into a rage.

So you see how the attacks of your pathological critic feed into your anger problem. The worse you feel about yourself, and the more shame and vulnerability you carry, the more likely you are to cope using anger. Doing something about your anger requires that you also do something about the critic and all its judgments. There are three key steps you can take to overcome the influence of your critic:

1.   Find core qualities in yourself that you value.

2.   Practice acceptance.

3.   Reinforce healthy thinking.

Finding Core Qualities You Can Value

Deep down, you know there are good things inside you. You can draw on that for ammunition to fight the critic. So it's time to find out more about some of your positive core qualities. The following exercise will help you explore what's good about yourself.

Exercise: Core Qualities Inventory
Answer the following questions in the space provided, using one word or very brief descriptions of each quality.

1. Qualities in you that others have praised and appreciated:

[Space Left Intentionally Blank in the Original Source]

2. Qualities the person who loved you most appreciated in you:

[Space Left Intentionally Blank in the Original Source]

3. Qualities that helped you survive life's struggles, pain, and dangers:

[Space Left Intentionally Blank in the Original Source]

4. Qualities that helped you reach certain life goals:

[Space Left Intentionally Blank in the Original Source]

5. Qualities that allowed you to help or bring happiness to others:

[Space Left Intentionally Blank in the Original Source]

6. Qualities that helped you at times feel happy, proud, or good about yourself:

[Space Left Intentionally Blank in the Original Source]

7. Things you're good at...

with your romantic partner:

[Space Left Intentionally Blank in the Original Source]

with your children:

[Space Left Intentionally Blank in the Original Source]

with your family/friends:

[Space Left Intentionally Blank in the Original Source]

at work/school:

[Space Left Intentionally Blank in the Original Source]

sports, hobbies, recreation:

[Space Left Intentionally Blank in the Original Source]

creativity, crafts, etc.:

[Space Left Intentionally Blank in the Original Source]

taking care of your home and home environments:

[Space Left Intentionally Blank in the Original Source]

taking care of yourself:

[Space Left Intentionally Blank in the Original Source]

Now carefully review the list of personal qualities you developed in this exercise. Write the top three, the ones you believe most and feel best about, in the space below:

[Space Left Intentionally Blank in the Original Source]

Exercise: Active Integration

It isn't enough to recognize positive qualities in yourself. You must actively work to keep them in mind. One strategy for increasing awareness of core qualities is called active integration. This involves each day finding an example from your past for up to three of your positive qualities. Here's how Emily, an out-of-work accountant, used active integration for three of her core qualities.

Date: 6/13
Quality 1: **caring.** I visited my grandmother daily when she was in the hospital last spring.

Quality 2: **take risks.** The time I asked Rick out, even though I'd just met him in a supermarket.

Quality 3: **lighthearted.** I kind of make people feel more up, like getting everybody laughing at Lisa's birthday party.

Date: 6/14
Quality 1: **caring.** When I went right over to Jason's house to comfort him after his mother

announced she was divorcing his dad.

Quality 2: **take risks.** I told my boss about some problems with his leadership style.

Quality 3: **lighthearted.** Even after that skiing accident, I was still joking with everyone and not

getting all down about it.

We suggest you make photocopies of the following worksheet so you can begin finding examples of your own positive core qualities. Try to remember examples of three qualities each day. Start with your top three from the Core Qualities Inventory. Keep working on them for several days to a week, and then move on to three other core qualities from the inventory.

ACTIVE INTEGRATION—Worksheet

Date: _____

Quality 1:

[Space Left Intentionally Blank in the Original Source]

Quality 2:

[Space Left Intentionally Blank in the Original Source]

Quality 3:

[Space Left Intentionally Blank in the Original Source]

Date: _____

Quality 1:

[Space Left Intentionally Blank in the Original Source]

Quality 2:

[Space Left Intentionally Blank in the Original Source]

Quality 3:

[Space Left Intentionally Blank in the Original Source]

Exercise: Affirm Your Worth

Go back over the Core Qualities Inventory, and in the space below write a summary of the main positive qualities you uncovered. Also include some of the situations or relationships where that quality is manifested:

[Space Left Intentionally Blank in the Original Source]

Emily's core qualities summary looked like this:

"I'm a sunny, lighthearted person who cheers people around me. I'm supportive and caring, particularly when people are sick or hurting. I give people courage when they're scared, and I show them how to face situations through my own example. I take risks to achieve goals. I'm a good athlete, an honest and loyal friend, and a terrific (as yet unpublished) writer of children's stories. I have a good aesthetic sense and know how to make myself attractive."

Read your core qualities summary over each morning. Make it part of your daily rituals so that the words become incredibly familiar, even memorized. The idea is to use the summary as an affirmation of qualities that you need to remember and cherish in yourself.

Practice Acceptance

The key to self-acceptance is to recognize that you're doing the best you can. This is hard to remember sometimes because the pathological critic would rather have you believe that you are willfully screwing up, making one deliberate mistake after another. The facts are quite different. If you went back, with an open mind, to explore the actual process by which you made a regrettable decision, you'd find that you made the choice that seemed best at the time.

Exercise: People Doing the Best They Can
This exercise can be found in chapter 6, p.53. The idea is to explore all the influences on your behavior

and choices, including your needs, fears, stresses, personal history, and a host of other factors. Go through this exercise for several unfortunate acts or choices and take an honest look at everything that influenced you. After you do, we believe that you may revise some of your judgments. You may, in fact, discover that mistakes are something you can only see in hindsight. At the moment the choice is made, it feels right. It feels like the thing you have to do. There may be doubts, but you go ahead, hoping and expecting that things will turn out okay.

Exercise: Ending Negative Self-Labels

In the left-hand column below, write all the negative labels your critic slings at you—ugly, dumb, loser, etc. Think back over the past few months to times when you felt particularly down on yourself. What was the critic telling you? What pejorative word or phrase did the critic use to describe your behavior? (Table 15.1)

ENDING NEGATIVE LABELS—Worksheet

Negative Labels	Alternative Thinking (Accurate and specific, balancing realities)
1.	1.
2.	2.
3.	3.
4.	4.
5.	5.

6.   6.

Table 15.1

Now, in the column headed Alternative Thinking, it's time to revise some of these hurtful labels. First of all, the label is far too global. Make it accurate and specific. How often do you behave this way? Once a week? Once a month? Once in a lifetime? What exactly *is* the problem or undesirable behavior? Describe it specifically. If, for example, the label is "stupid," how often do you act this way? What exactly, behaviorally, does stupid mean? That the checkbook is seven dollars out of balance? That you forgot the PTA meeting twice in the last year? That you told a friend about a problem that you wish you hadn't? The point is to define carefully what these negative words are supposed to be describing.

Also, under Alternative Thinking, note any balancing realities—positive things you do that counterweight the negative. For example, you're often awkward in conversation with strangers, but are warm and engaging talking to friends. Or you have several nasty fights a year with your mother, but are faithful about calls and visits.

The first items on Emily's Ending Negative Labels Worksheet looked like this: (Table 15.2)

ENDING NEGATIVE LABELS—Example

Negative Labels	Alternative Thinking (Accurate and specific, balancing realities)
1. foolish and impulsive	1. Basically this means I bought several outfits I shouldn't have for about $350 total. On the other hand, I'm paying the card down and looked great at the reunion.
2. airhead	2. I got in trouble three times at last job for math mistakes, but they also said I had a good knowledge of tax law.
3. self-centered bitch	3. My brother's line. I think a lot about my appearance and my own needs; I am also generous with my time and support to friends, and family.

Table 15.2

From now on, any time you catch yourself using a negative label, challenge it. Turn it into a statement that's specific and accurate, and find other, positive qualities that balance it.

Reinforce Healthy Thinking

Softening and changing negative judgments takes committed effort. One way to maintain that commitment is to make a contract with a friend or family member. Write down on a piece of paper what you're planning to do (i.e., active integration, affirming your worth, or ending negative labels). Commit yourself to one or more of these efforts for a specific period of time. Sign the contract and give it to your friend or family member. Ask them to check in with you regularly about your progress dealing with the critic.

A second strategy for reinforcing healthy thinking is to use a system of rewards. Each time you revise a negative label, give yourself a treat. It might be reading the next chapter in an exciting book, renting a video, or calling a good friend. After affirming your worth each morning, make sure you have a really delicious breakfast or have time to read the paper and enjoy your coffee. Think of these pleasant activities as a reward for remembering your core positive qualities.

Nourish Yourself

There are three main components to self-nourishment: physical comfort, connectedness, and emotional balance. The Self-Nourishment Checklist that follows is an opportunity to review a variety of activities that might be beneficial to include in your daily life. Put a check mark by each item that might improve the quality of your life.

Self-Nourishment Checklist
Physical Comfort
_ Temperature/Warmth

Keeping optimal room temperature; hot showers or tubs

_ Clothes

Pleasing texture and color; loose rather than constricting

_ Bed

Good support; warm and comforting

_ Furniture

At least one good, comfortable chair; a work space with room to spread out

_ Food

Healthy, good-tasting foods to look forward to

_ Drink

Warm or cool, good-tasting beverages; avoid caffeine

_ Massage/Sensuality

Relaxing physical touch

_ Tension Level

> Relaxation exercises; meditation

_ Energy

> Rest; sleep; quiet time

_ Movement

> Aerobic exercises; stretching; athletics

_ Pain Level

> If pain can be remedied, get immediate treatment or something to soothe it

_ Smell

> Avoid unpleasant odors; consider using scents

_ Grooming

> Manicure, haircuts, etc.

_ Pace of life

> Avoid rushing—plan space between appointments and events; generous deadlines

Connectedness

_ Friends

Regular contact through phone and visits; plan shared activities

_ Groups

Sense of belonging to a regularly scheduled group activity: sports, hobbies, political or community action, educational or creative groups, etc.

_ Family

Regular contact with supportive and interested family members

_ Generosity

Giving and doing things for others

_ Partner

Creating time alone with each other; scheduling fun; planning sensual or sexual experiences; small gifts (objects or time and energy)

_ Community

Church activities; PTA; town hall; neighborhood association

Emotional Balance
_ Meaning

Setting and pursuing a goal; service to others; creating something

_ Pleasure

Scheduling time for things you enjoy

_ Limits

Saying no to things you don't want to do or experience

_ Gratitude

Daily meditation on what you appreciate and value in your life

_ Mindfulness

Disciplining your mind to focus on the moment—what it feels like to wash the dishes, drive with the window open, take long strides as you walk home; mindfulness meditation

_ Creativity

Making things—whether poetry and art or hemming new curtains

_ Aesthetics

Arranging your environment so there are more things you like to look at

_ Nature

Planning regular periods (however brief) in your favorite natural environments

_ Learning

Enjoying new knowledge; developing a new skill

_ Affirmation

Reminding yourself regularly of your positive core qualities (see Affirming Your Worth in this chapter)

_ Time alone

Scheduling private time to think, reflect, and plan

_ Stress breaks

> Scheduling brief recovery periods (from a few minutes to a few days) to help manage stressful situations

_ After-work cool-out

> Time to decompress immediately after getting home

_ Passive relaxation

> Books, videos, plays, etc.

_ Active relaxation

> Hobbies, interests, projects

Having completed the checklist, it's time to go back and circle the three self-nourishment activities you want to try first. With this accomplished, you can move on to the next section—making a self-nourishment plan. It's not enough to want to do something. You have to plan for it and integrate it's into your life.

Exercise: Self-Nourishment Plan
Item 1 _____

When (day/time) _____

Where _____

Frequency (if applicable) _____

Rescheduling (what do you have to change or arrange or stop doing to make room for this self-nourishment experience?)

[Space Left Intentionally Blank in the Original Source]

Item 2 _____

When (day/time) _____

Where _____

Frequency (if applicable) _____

Rescheduling (what do you have to change or arrange or stop doing to make room for this self-nourishment experience?)

[Space Left Intentionally Blank in the Original Source]

Item 3 _____

When (day/time) _____

Where _____

Frequency (if applicable) _____

Rescheduling (what do you have to change or arrange or stop doing to make room for this self-nourishment experience?)

[Space Left Intentionally Blank in the Original Source]

CHAPTER 16

GETTING UNSTUCK

Sometimes, no matter how hard you've worked on anger management skills, a provocative situation will get the best of you. It can be discouraging—and costly, particularly if your temper pushes you into some seriously aggressive or destructive behavior.

Don't give up. If you look back over your Anger Logs, you'll see a lot of ups and downs over the weeks. There are flare-ups; then there are periods when you are coping more effectively. There are also particular provocations that are clearly harder than others. So if you've been charting your progress, you would see a "sawtooth" profile. On *average,* though, despite the setbacks, you are probably angry less often and less intensely than you were at the start of this program.

That said, what can you do now if some provocation really gets to you? Or if a problem or conflict has become chronically upsetting? There are four things you can do.

Use your Anger Plans Worksheet

Go back to chapter 13, "Your Plan for Real-life Coping," and complete the Anger Plans Worksheet for any provocation that gets the better of you. This is important. Planning is 50 percent of anger management; the other 50 percent is practice. Find out what trigger thoughts are seducing you into a blowup. Look for or develop coping thoughts (see Best Coping Thoughts Worksheet) that are specific antidotes for your anger triggers. And while you're at it, plan one or two coping behaviors that help you disengage from the upset.

Identify and Cope with the Feelings Underneath Your Anger

One function of anger, as you learned in chapter 3, is to cover or cope with emotional pain. Anger tends to block awareness of feelings such as shame, fear, or hurt. It's like a great big boulder that obscures a lot of your emotional landscape.

If anger usually gets the upper hand with certain provocations, it often means that the anger is highly reinforced because it protects you from some other feeling—a feeling you'd prefer not to face. Overcoming anger in this situation may necessitate identifying that underlying feeling and finding an alternative way to cope with it.

Exercise: What's Underneath the Anger

Visualize a recent provocation where your anger got the upper hand. Close your eyes and form an image of the setting—colors, shapes, sounds, smells, and physical sensations such as heat or texture. Notice who's there and listen to what's being said. Also notice any trigger thoughts you may have. Take some time to really anchor yourself in the scene.

Now hit the rewind button and go back to the beginning, just as your anger was getting started. And then keep going a little further back—before the trigger thoughts and the anger—to what you first felt. Notice your inner climate at that moment. Stay with it. Take a few deep breaths and try to capture the emotion.

Now look at the following list to see if any of these feelings were present *before* the anger hit:

- Guilt—a sense of having done something wrong.

- Shame—a deep feeling of being unacceptable, flawed, or contemptible.

- Hurt—a feeling of being devalued or denigrated by others.

- Loss—a feeling that something you needed or counted on is lost or missing.

- Hunger/Frustrated Drive—an aching for something; a strong sense of incompleteness.

- Helplessness—the feeling that there's nothing you can do about your pain; crucial elements of your life are beyond your control.

- Anxiety/Fear—a dread of something that could happen; a sense of danger; a fear of certain things or situations.

- Feeling Unworthy—a sense that you aren't good enough, that you are bad or wrong or without intrinsic value.

- Emptiness—a sense either of numbness or a hollowness that requires constant attention and activity.

Three Strategies to Cope with Painful Feelings
If you've identified one of the above emotions as present just before your anger surged, chances are the anger was functioning as a breakwater to keep the feeling from overwhelming you. Now there is an

important task ahead: You need to find an alternative way to cope with this feeling *besides anger.* There are three basic strategies to manage painful emotions.

One is to simply accept and "hold" the feeling for a while. It won't last forever. A common delusion when we're in pain is that there will never be an end to it. If you think back to struggles with similar emotions, you know that even the hardest ones to bear are time limited—eventually they pass. So notice the wave hit, crest, and gradually recede. Take some deep breaths. Imagine the pain is next to you, not *in you,* or see it from a distance. Give it a color and shape. Watch while it slowly, slowly shrinks in size.

The second strategy is to use coping thoughts, just like you've learned to do with anger. Begin by noticing the thoughts that trigger your feeling. What are you saying to yourself that intensifies the pain? Write these thoughts down. Now *rewrite* the negative thoughts following these key rules:

- Make the thoughts *accurate* rather than exaggerated.

- Make the thoughts *specific* rather than general.

- Use nonpejorative language.

- Include balancing realities and alternative explanations. Ask yourself what's the positive part of the picture that you're leaving out?

The following three self-help books are recommended for developing coping thoughts in response to a wide variety of painful feelings:

- *Thoughts and Feelings: Getting Control of Your Moods and Your Life* by Matthew McKay, Martha Davis, and Patrick Fanning

- *Mind Over Mood* by Dennis Greenburger and Christine Pedesky

- *Feeling Good: The New Mood Therapy* by David Burns

The third strategy for coping with difficult feelings is to develop a problem-solving plan. What can you change in your life, in your relationships, or in your behavior to diminish this painful feeling? If you stop the angry blaming, maybe there is something *you* can do to make things different. Begin by writing out a clearly stated goal. Now brainstorm some alternative solutions. List as many as you can think of. Quantity is better than quality. Don't evaluate your ideas, just generate a lot of them.

After you've listed between ten and twenty alternative solutions, try to rule out the obviously unworkable ones. For the solutions that remain, list the positive and negative consequences for each one. Try to identify both the short- and long-term outcomes. Finally, select one or more alternative solution that you would like to try. Be sure to decide on a first step toward implementation—including when and where you'll take it.

So whether you're afraid of something, or feeling helpless and stuck, or yearning for something you don't have, problem solving may help you to create real changes in the situation.

Example: Ricardo's Vacation

To illustrate the value of problem solving for anger control, consider Ricardo's struggle to take needed time off from his interior design business. He's irritable, exhausted, plus he wants to spend time with his mother in New Mexico. Problem is, he has a one-man office. He's afraid of alienating his clients and dropping the ball on some important projects if he takes time off.

Ricardo started with the clear goal: "I want two weeks both to relax and spend time with my mother." While brainstorming solutions, he came up with fourteen ideas ranging from "carry blueprints with me and conduct business by e-mail" to "send clients some French Chardonnay and tell them to chill for two weeks."

Ricardo listed positive and negative consequences for his top three solutions. For example, "get a cell phone hook-up in Gallup to talk to clients" had some clear advantages and disadvantages: (Table 16.1)

Advantages	Disadvantages
Can "put out fires" at work	Expense
Stay in touch with key clients	Vacation can be interrupted any time
	Never really relax
	Feel cheated

Table 16.1

Ricardo finally settled on the following idea: "Take two week-long vacations separated by a brief catch-up period." He planned to make no calls while he was gone, except emergencies. Decision made, Ricardo immediately called his travel agent.

Identify the Anger Payoffs

Something others do in response to your anger may be reinforcing it. Anger can be an effective coercive strategy. People back off or give in when you get angry. You end up getting your way, and anger gives you a temporary feeling of control.

In the long run, of course, people get inured to your anger and resistant to coercion. They stop giving in and just go away. But in a particular relationship or situation, anger may still be quite rewarding, and it may be hard for you to give up such a reliable tool for getting things to go the way you want.

Exercise: What's Reinforcing the Anger?

On the worksheet below, identify three recent anger situations where you got upset and would like to change your behavior in the future. In the middle column of the worksheet, identify the positive outcomes from your anger response in each situation. In other words, what did people do that you wanted them to do? How did people react to your anger that was beneficial or rewarding for you? What short-term positive changes came about as a result of your blowup? In the right-hand column of the worksheet, identify an alternative coping strategy that might have yielded the same result—for example, an assertive statement about your needs and feelings. Or a clear, but non-hostile, statement about your limits in the situation. Or efforts toward negotiation. Or making your own coping plan (independent of others) to change the situation. We've included a sample worksheet filled out by Ronnie, a thirty-six-year-old single woman living with a room-mate.

This worksheet can be an important resource for identifying anger reinforcers and finding an alter-native way to get your needs met. Whenever you're puzzled by an anger response that seems hard to change, do this simple three-step analysis to see how your anger is being rewarded, and how you can get the same reward using strategies that don't damage your relationships.

Make a Contract

In chapter 1, you started your anger management program by making a twenty-four-hour promise to behave calmly. That was a helpful exercise because it taught you that you could control your anger—one day at a time. This is an opportunity to make a different kind of contract. Instead of agreeing to stay calm for twenty-four hours, you are going to promise a particular individual that you will never engage in a specific target behavior with them again. For example, if you have an ongoing problem of name-calling with a particular person, and you believe this behavior is damaging and needs to change, you can sign a contract to do so.

The contract (a sample can be found at the end of the chapter) has five provisions. First, it is a promise made to a particular individual. Second, it should contain a clear description of the target anger behavior. It's best if the contract focuses on *one behavior only.* Promising too much, and trying to remember too much, will sabotage your effort. Third, the contract should identify a signal that the other person can use to warn you when your target behavior is starting. The signal should be clearly described and defined. Fourth, there should be a provision to stop everything and take a time-out as soon as you see the signal. This means that you don't say another word. You shut up and the issue is dropped until you can talk about it more calmly later on. Fifth, the contract should identify at least two other support people who know and care about your promise. They may sign the contract as witnesses, but at the very least, they should agree to check in with you periodically about your promise.(Image 16.1, 16.2)

You're a Whole Lot Stronger Than You Used to Be

It takes two things to change. First, you need determination—you need a big reason and a strong resolve. The fact that you've read this far means that you've got the determination to make a real change in your life.

WHAT'S REINFORCING THE ANGER—Worksheet		
Anger Situation	Positive Outcomes	Alternative Coping
1		
2		
3		

Image 16.1

Second, you need skills. This book has given you the skills. Every time you successfully control your anger, you get stronger. It's like a muscle that develops each time you exercise it. You've been doing anger management "push-ups" for weeks or months now. In the beginning, it took everything you had, every fiber of your resolve, to remember to breathe and relax and use your coping thoughts. More and more, this has become second nature, and it isn't so hard now because the anger management muscle is strong and buffed. Keep at it. Don't neglect your skills. Don't forget to breathe and cope. The quality of your life, and the lives of those you love, are so much better because you've done this work.

WHAT'S REINFORCING THE ANGER—
Ronnie's Worksheet

Anger Situation	Positive Outcomes	Alternative Coping
1 Boss dumps huge pile of work on my desk at 4:30 and says he needs it by tomorrow. I get angry and sarcastic.	He gives half of it to someone else.	Assertively explain that I can only work till 6:30. So if he wants it done, someone else will have to help
2 Melinda (close friend) asks if it's okay if she goes out with my ex. I explode, call her "someone with an instinct for betrayal."	Melinda apologizes. Calls Jeff (my ex) and tells him he should never have asked.	Share my feelings without blaming her. Explain that it hurts too much to see him happily dating my best friend, and that it could distance us.
3 Roommate wakes me up when she comes in, loud and rowdy with her boyfriend. Scream, "Shut up, you F---heads."	They cool it, she stops bringing him home.	Come in the living room and ask calmly. Negotiate an evening quiet time—say after 11 P.M.

Image 16.2

ANGER CONTRACT

I _____, on this date commit myself to _____ that I will never engage in the following anger

behavior with him/her:

Description of behavior: (one behavior only)

332

[Space Left Intentionally Blank in the Original Source]

I will watch for the following signal, to be given at the first sign of the anger behavior:

[Space Left Intentionally Blank in the Original Source]

Whenever the signal is given, I will stop talking and end the discussion until I'm calm enough to deal with it. I will absolutely, positively cease the target behavior. There are at least two other people who know about my promise and will check in with me to help me keep it. Their names are:

[Space Left Intentionally Blank in the Original Source]

_____ (Your Signature)

_____ (Witness)

_____ (Witness)

APPENDIX

RESEARCH ON THE EFFECTS OF ANGER

Physiological Costs of Anger

Anger and Hypertension

The following studies have shown the connection between unexpressed anger(anger-in) and hypertension:

Alexander, F. 1939. Emotional factors in hypertension. *Psychosomatic Medicine* 1:175–179.

Diamond, E.L. 1982. The role of anger and hostility in essential hypertension and coronary heart disease. *Psychological Bulletin* 92:410–433.

Dimsdale, J.E., C. Pierce, D. Schoenfeld, A. Brown. 1986. Suppressed anger and blood pressure: The effects of race, sex, social class, obesity, and age. *Psychosomatic Medicine* 48:430–436.

Esler, M.S., S. Julius, A. Zweifler, O. Randall, E. Harburg, H. Gardiner, and E. De Quattro. 1977. Mild high-rennin essential hypertension: Neurogenic human hypertension? *New England Journal of Medicine* 296:405–411.

Gentry, W.D. 1982. Habitual anger-coping styles: Effect on mean blood pressure and risk for essential hypertension. *Psychosomatic Medicine* 44:195–202.

Hamilton, J.A. 1942. Psychophysiology of blood pressure. *Psychosomatic Medicine* 4:125–133

Harburg, E., J.C. Erfurt, L.S. Hauenstein, C. Chape, W.J. Schull, and M.A. Schork. 1973. Socio-ecological stress, suppressed hostility, skin color, and black-white male blood pressure: Detroit. *Psychosomatic Medicine* 35:2726–296.

Kahn, H.A., J.H. Medalie, H.N. Newfield, E. Riss, and U. Goldbourt. 1972. The incidence of hypertension and associated factors: The Israel ischemic heart disease study. *American Heart Journal* 84:171–182.

Miller, C., and C. Grim. 1979. Personality and emotional stress measurement on hypertensive patients with essential and secondary hypertension. *International Journal of Nursing Studies* 16:85–93.

Thomas, S.P. 1997. Women's anger: relationship of suppression to blood pressure. *Nursing Research* 46:324–30.

Additional Annotated Studies

Harburg, E., S. Julius, N.F. McGinn, J. McLeod, and S.W. Hoobler. 1964. Personality traits and behavior patterns associated with systolic blood pressure levels in college males. *Journal of Chronic Diseases* 17:405–414. Harburg and associates demonstrated the correlation between high blood pressure and hypertension in a college population.

Van der Ploeg, H.M., E.T. Van Buuren, and P. Van Brummelen. 1985. The role of anger in hypertension. *Psychotherapy & Psychosomatics* 43:186–193. Van der Ploeg and associates studied 208 subjects in the Netherlands. Their results supported a psychosomatic theory of hypertension, and found that hypertensives tend to avoid showing anger.

The following studies have shown the connection between expressed anger(anger-out) and

hypertension:

Baer, P.E., F.H. Collins, G.C. Bourianoff, and M.F. Ketchel. 1983. Assessing personality factors in essential hypertension with a brief self-report instrument. *Psychosomatic Medicine* 45:59–63.

Harburg, E., E.H. Blakelock, and P.J. Roeper. 1979. Resentful and reflective coping with arbitrary authority and blood pressure: Detroit. *Psychosomatic Medicine* 41:189–202.

Kaplan, S., L.A. Gottschalk, E. Magliocco, D. Rohovit, and W. Ross. 1961. Hostility in verbal productions and hypnotic dreams in hypertensive patients. *Psychosomatic Medicine* 23:311–322.

Mann, A.H. 1977. Psychiatric morbidity and hostility in hypertension. *Psychological Medicine* 7:653–659.

Schachter, J. 1957. Pain, fear, and anger in hypertensives and normotensives. *Psychosomatic Medicine* 19:17–29.

Anger, Hostility and Cardiovascular Disease

The following studies have shown the connection between anger, hostility and various forms of cardio-vascular disease:

Barefoot, J.C., W.G. Dahlstrom, and R.B. Williams, Jr. 1983. Hostility, CHD incidence, and total morbidity: a 25–year follow-up study of 255 physicians. *Psychosomatic Medicine* 45:59–63.

Barefoot, J.C., T.L. Haney, R.R. Harper, T.M. Dembroski, and R.B. Williams, Jr. 1990. Interview assessed hostility and the severity of coronary artery disease. Paper presented at the 98th Annual Convention of the APA. Boston MA.

Friedman, M. and R.H. Rosenman. 1974. *Type A Behavior and Your Heart.* New York: Alfred A. Knopf.

Grunnbaum, J.A., S.W. Vernon, and C.M. Clasen. 1997. The association between anger and hostility and risk factors for coronary heart disease in children and adolescents: a review. *Annals of Behavioral Medicine* 19:179–189.

Kawachi, I., D. Sparrow, A. Spiro, P. Vokonas, and S.T. Weiss. 1996. A prospective study of anger and coronary heart disease. The Normative Aging Study. *Circulation* 94:2090–2095.

Rosenman, R.H. 1985. Health consequences of anger and implications for treatment. In *Anger and Hostility in Cardiovascular and Behavioral Disorders,* edited by M.A. Chesny and R.H. Rosenman. Washington DC: Hemisphere Publishing Co.

Shekelle, R.B., M. Gale, A.M. Ostfeld, and O. Paul. 1983. Hostility, risk of coronary heart disease, and mortality. *Psychosomatic Medicine* 45:109–114.

Siegman, A.W., T.M. Dembroski, and N. Ringel. 1987. Components of hostility and severity of coronary artery disease. *Psychosomatic Medicine* 49:127–135.

Additional Annotated Studies

Joesoef, M.R., S.F. Wetterhall, F. DeStefano, N.E. Stroup, and A. Fronek. 1989. The association of peripheral arterial disease with hostility in a young, healthy population. *Psychosomatic Medicine* 51:285–289. In a cross-sectional study of U.S. army veterans, Joesoef and associates found that those with higher hostility scores were more likely to have peripheral artery disease.

Ricci, B., E. Pio, P. Gremgni, G. Bertolotti, and A.M. Zotti. 1995. Dimensions of anger and hostility in cardiac patients, hypertensive patients, and controls. 64:162–172. Ricci and associates studied 240 patients in Italy. They found that the frequency and extent to which people experienced anger arousal had pathogenic effects. Specifically, their results indicate that the more aggressively people tend to respond, the more likely they are to experience coronary heart disease.

Williams, R.B., T.L. Haney, K.I. Lee, J. Kong, J.A. Blumenthal, and R.E. Walen. 1980. Type A behavior, hostility, and coronary atherosclerosis. *Psychosomatic Medicine* 42:539–549. Williams and associates, testing 424 patients referred for coronary angiography (X-rays of the heart's blood supply), found that 70 percent of those with higher hostility scores had significant atherosclerosis.

Anger, Hostility, and Death from All Causes

The following studies have shown the connection between anger, hostility and total mortality:

Chesney, M.A., M. Hecker, and G.W. Black. 1989. Coronary-prone components of Type A behavior in the WGSC: A new methodology. In *Type A Behavior Pattern: Research, Theory, and Intervention,* edited by B.K. Houston and C.R. Snyder. New York: Wiley.

Koskenvuo, M. J. Kaprio, R.J. Rose, A. Kasaniemi, K. Heikkila, and H. Langinvainio. 1988. Hostility as a risk factor for mortality and ischemic heart disease in men. *Psychosomatic Medicine* 50:330–340.

Schekelle, R.B., M. Gale, A.M. Ostfeld, and O. Paul. 1983. Hostility, risk of coronary heart disease, and mortality. *Psychosomatic Medicine* 45:109–114.

Additional Annotated Studies

Carmelli, D., G.E. Swan, R.H. Rosenman, M.H. Hecker, and D.R. Ragland. 1989. Behavioral components and total mortality in the WGSC. Paper presented at the meeting of the Society of Behavioral Medicine. San Francisco, CA. Carmelli and associates found that anger scores predicted total mortality over a 22–year follow-up period.

340

Carmody, T.P., J.R. Crossen, and A.N. Wiens. 1989. Hostility as a risk factor: Relationships with neuroticism, Type A behavior, attentional focus, and interpersonal style. *Journal of Clinical Psychology* 45:754–762. Carmody and associates studied 2204 psychologically normal and physically healthy males, aged 20–43. Their findings support the idea that hostility is one dimension of the disease-prone personality.

Deshields, T., J.O. Jenkins, and R.C. Tait. 1989. The experience of anger in chronic illness: A preliminary investigation. *International Journal of Psychiatry in Medicine* 19:299–309. Deshields and associates reported that the chronic patient groups they studied differed significantly from the nonpatient control group. The chronic patient group reported more anger in general and a greater frequency of anger experiences. They also reported greater severity of health problems.

Emotional and Interpersonal Costs of Anger and Hostility

The following studies have shown the connection between anger, hostility and less satisfactory social supports. This section also includes studies relating to damaged friendships, increased fights with family members, and difficulties at school or in the workplace.

Blumenthal, J.A., J.C. Barefoot, M.M. Burg, and R.B. Williams, Jr. 1987. Psychological correlates of hostility among patients undergoing coronary angiography. *British Journal of Medical Psychology* 60:349–355.

Deffenbacher, J.L. 1992. Trait anger: Theory, findings, and implications. In Spielberger, C.D. and Butcher, J.N. (Eds.) *Advances in Personality Assessment.* 177–201. Lawrence Erlbaum Associates, Inc. Hillsdale, NJ.

Greenglass, E.R. 1996. Anger suppression, cynical distrust, and hostility: Implications for coronary heart disease. In Spielberger, C.D. and Sarason, I.G. (Eds.) *Stress and emotion: Anxiety, anger and curiosity.* 205–225.

Hansson, R.D., W.H. Jones, and B. Carpenter. 1984. Relational competence and social support. *Review of Personality and Social Psychology* 5:265–284.

Hardy, J.D. and T.W. Smith. 1988. Cynical hostility and vulnerability to disease: Social support, life stress, and physiological response to conflict. *Health Psychology* 7:447–459.

Hazaleus, S., and J. Deffenbacher. 1986. Relaxation and cognitive treatments of anger. *Journal of Consulting and Clinical Psychology* 54:222–226.

Houston, B.K., and K.E. Kelley. 1989. Hostility in employed women: Relation to work and marital experiences, social support, stress, and anger expression. *Personality and Social Psychology Bulletin* 15:175–182.

Jones, W.H., J.E. Freeman, and R.A. Gasewick. 1981. The persistence of loneliness: Self and other determinants. *Journal of Personality* 49:27–48.

Liebsohn, M.T., E.R. Oetting, and J.L. Deffenbacher. 1994. The effects of trait anger on alcohol consumption and consequences. *Journal of Adolescent Substance Abuse* 3:17–32.

Smith, T.W., and K.D. Frohm. 1985. What's so healthy about hostility? Construct validity and psychosocial correlates of the Cook & Medley Ho scale. *Health Psychology* 4:503–520.

Smith, T.W., M.K. Pope, J.D. Sanders, J.D. Allred, and J.L. O'Keeffe. Cynical hostility at home and work: Psychosocial vulnerability across domains. *Journal of Research in Personality* 22:525–548.

Additional Annotated Studies

In this series of articles, Deffenbacher and associates, using primarily college students and adolescents as subjects, studied people who identified anger as a personal problem. They selected those subjects who scored in the upper quartile on Spielberger's Trait Anger Scale. This sample was found to express their anger in outward, negative, and poorly controlled ways. The research suggests that these individuals were more likely to suffer damaged friendships, as well as having more fights with family members.

Deffenbacher, J.L., R. Lynch, E.R. Oetting, and C.C. Kemper. Anger reduction in early adolescents. *Journal of Counseling Psychology* 43:149–157.

Deffenbacher, J.L., E.R. Oetting, M.E. Huff, and G.R. Cornell. Evaluation of two cognitive-behavioral approaches to general anger reduction. *Cognitive Therapy and Research* 20:551–573.

Deffenbacher, J.L., E.R. Oetting, R.S. Lynch, and C.D. Morris. 1996. The expression of anger and its consequences. *Behavior research and Therapy* 34:575–590.

Deffenbacher, J.L., E.R. Oetting, G.A. Thwaites, R.S. Lynch, D.A. Baker, R.S. Stark, S. Thacker, and L. Eiswerth-Cox. 1996. State-Trait anger theory and the utility of the Trait Anger Scale. *Journal of Counseling Psychology* 43:131–148.

Deffenbacher, J.L., and P.M. Sabadell. 1990. A combination of cognitive, relaxation, and behavioral coping skills in the reduction of general anger. *Journal of College Student Development* 31:351–358.

SUGGESTED READINGS

Beck, A. 1999. *Prisoners of Hate: The Cognitive Basis of Anger, Hostility & Violence.* New York: HarperCollins.

Burns, D. 1980. *Feeling Good: The New Mood Therapy.* New York: William Morrow.

Davis, M., E.R. Eshelman, and M. McKay. 1998. *Relaxation and Stress Reduction Workbook* (Fourth Edition). Oakland, CA: New Harbinger Publications.

Deschner, J.P. 1984. *The Hitting Habit.* New York: The Free Press, Macmillan Publishers.

Ellis, A. 1998. *How to Control Your Anger Before It Controls You.* Secaucus, NJ: Carol Publishing Group.

Greenberger, D. and C.A. Pedesky. 1995. *Mind Over Mood.* New York: Guilford Press. Lerner, H.G. 1985. *The Dance of Anger.* New York: Harper & Row.

McKay, M., M. Davis, and P. Fanning. 1998. *Thoughts and Feelings* Second Edition. Oakland, CA.: New Harbinger Publications.

McKay, M., K. Paleg, P. Fanning, and D. Landis. 1996. *When Anger Hurts Your Kids.* Oakland, CA New Harbinger Publications.

McKay, M., P.D. Rogers, and J. McKay. 1987. *When Anger Hurts.* Oakland, CA.: New Harbinger Publications.

McKay, M., P.D. Rogers, J.D. Blades, and R. Gosse. 1999. *The Divorce Book.* Oakland, CA: New Harbinger Publications.

Neidig, P.H. and D.H. Friedman. 1984. *Spouse Abuse: A treatment Program for Couples.* Champaign, IL: Research Press.

Potter-Efron, R. 1994. *Angry All the Time.* Oakland, CA.: New Harbinger Publications.

Tavris, C. 1989. *Anger: The Misunderstood Emotion.* New York: Simon & Schuster.

For Therapists:

Deffenbacher, J.L. and M. McKay. 2000. *Overcoming Situational and General Anger (Therapist Protocol).* Oakland, CA: New Harbinger Publications.

Matthew McKay, Ph.D., is the Clinical Director of Haight-Ashbury Psychological Services in San Francisco. Dr. McKay is the coauthor of thirteen popular books, including *The Relaxation & Stress Reduction Workbook, When Anger Hurts, Couple Skills, Thoughts & Feelings, When Anger Hurts Your Kids, Self-Esteem,* and several professional titles.

Peter Rogers, Ph.D. is the Administrative Director of Haight-Ashbury Psychological Services in San Francisco, and the past Director of the Alcohol and Drug Treatment Program at Kaiser Permanente in Redwood City, California. Dr. Rogers is coauthor of *The Divorce Book* and *When Anger Hurts,* and author of book chapters and articles on alcohol and drug abuse.

Books For ALL Kinds of Readers

At ReadHowYouWant we understand that one size does not fit all types of readers. Our innovative, patent pending technology allows us to design new formats to make reading easier and more enjoyable for you. This helps improve your speed of reading and your comprehension. Our EasyRead printed books have been optimized to improve word recognition, ease eye tracking by adjusting word and line spacing as well as minimizing hyphenation. Our EasyRead SuperLarge editions have been developed to make reading easier and more accessible for vision-impaired readers. We offer Braille and DAISY formats of our books and all popular E-Book formats.

We are continually introducing new formats based upon research and reader preferences. Visit our web-site to see all of our formats and learn how you can Personalize our books for yourself or as gifts. Sign up to Become A RHYW Registered Reader.

www.readhowyouwant.com

Made in the USA
Monee, IL
22 September 2020